Coaching The Threads of Reading

Helping Teachers Build Reading Success

KAREN TANKERSLEY

Little John Publishing
Las Vegas, NV
https://threadsofreading.com

Little John Publishing
A Division of Southwest Training Development, Inc.
20118 North Sixty-seventh Avenue, Suite 300-159
Glendale, Arizona 85308, United States of America
https://www.threadsofreading.com

ISBN: 0615552307
ISBN-13: 9780615552309

Library of Congress Control Number: 2011940911
Little John Publishing Glendale, AZ

Table of Contents

4

"Literacy is not a luxury; it is a right and a responsibility. If our world is to meet the challenges of the twenty-first century, we must harness the energy and creativity of all our citizens."
President Clinton on International Literacy Day, September 8, 1994

Introduction

The Foundation of Effective Reading

A child's oral language development begins in the womb. It continues at an explosive rate during the first few years of life. When children reach the kindergarten door, the amount of oral language they possess—or lack—directly affects their probability of reading success (Hart & Risley, 1995; Shaywitz, 2003) during the K-3 school years. Over forty years ago, researchers discovered that children who entered school with strong oral language skills and a well-developed vocabulary became the most proficient readers and writers (Durkin, 1966; Loban, 1976).

Although other factors can prevent reading success, current research (Dickinson & Tabors, 2001) continues to stress this essential link between a child's background and their ability to become a successful reader. Children who come to school with a rich and extensive vocabulary and who have had experience with books and writing from those first five years of life will have a solid foundation upon which to build new understandings about reading and writing. Those from impoverished backgrounds where books and words are not a daily priority will have more difficulty becoming strong and proficient readers and writers.

For a much deeper explanation of how children learn to read, see *The Threads of Reading: Strategies for Literacy Development* (Tankersley, 2003) or *Literacy Strategies for Grades 4-12: Reinforcing the Threads of Reading* (Tankersley, 2005). In these books, you will find a more detailed discussion of the research on becoming a proficient reader, developing oral language, enhancing and building vocabulary, and laying the foundation for solid reading success.

Reading in the Primary Grades

Helping young children get off to a good beginning with their reading experience in first grade is crucial to reading success for children. As Torgesen (2009) writes:

"We know, for example, that delayed development of reading skills affects vocabulary growth (Cunningham & Stanovich, 1998), alters children's attitudes and motivation to read (Oka & Paris, 1986), and leads to missed opportunities to develop comprehension strategies (Brown, Palinscar, & Purcell, 1986) If children fall seriously behind in the growth of critical early reading skills, they have fewer opportunities to practice reading. Recent evidence (Torgensen, Rashotte, & Alexander, 2001) suggests that these lost practice opportunities make it extremely difficult for children who remain poor readers during the first three years of elementary school to acquire average reading fluency. All of this explains the very sobering fact obtained from several longitudinal studies: Children who are poor readers at the end of first grade seldom acquire average-level reading skills by the end of elementary school (Francis, Shaywitz, Stuebing, Shaywitz, & Fletcher, 1996; Juel, 1988; Shaywitz et al.,1999; Torgesen & Burgess, 1998)" (p.1).

As a result of the importance of learning to read during those foundational kindergarten-to-3rd-grade years, children who are headed toward early reading failure must be identified and provided with intensive and targeted support as quickly as possible before they become hopelessly behind. Children must develop critical phonological skills to quickly and easily decode the words they encounter on the printed page to read well. As a result, the foundational key to success in learning to read is for the child to identify the letters by name; hear, distinguish, and blend individual sounds; and match sounds to print during their early years. This leads to acquiring a large bank of sight words and fluent and effortless reading.

This is a critical time that can make or break a child's potential for school success and good academic performance. Since effective and targeted instruction during the K-3 years is essential to reading success, we must have only the most knowledgeable teachers working with our beginning readers. Strong teachers, supported by strong reading coaches who can help them analyze and reflect on their instruction, are necessary to help children acquire the basic reading skills they can build on throughout life.

Young children know that school is where learning to read happens. Adults often tell them they must attend school to earn to read. As a result, many children, especially those whose home lives have been filled with books and parents who read to them, are excited to begin learning to read those wonderful books for themselves. When these children finally go to school, many expect they will instantly learn to read by the end of the first day of school.

At the end of the first week of school, my kindergarten daughter announced that she was disappointed that her teacher had still not taught her to read. She demanded to know when that vital bit of learning would take place. She was impatient to get this skill mastered so she didn't have to rely on others to read to her. She was motivated to read many story books whenever she wanted without adult help.

Despite her intense desire to learn to read quickly, it would take time to learn to read. I knew she didn't understand then that this critical process wouldn't happen quickly. No matter how much she wanted to read independently, learning to read would take time and lots of practice. It would take time to learn to translate the mysterious squiggles on the page into wonderful stories and poems that she could read and enjoy independently.

Looking back, I realize that this child was lucky. As a result of her rich experiences at home, she came to school with the background she needed to become a successful reader. The solid phonemic awareness skills she had developed and the strong instructional skills of her kindergarten and 1st-grade teachers helped the reading process come together for her. She learned the letters and their corresponding sounds quickly and, much to our delight, progressed well as a beginning reader.

In kindergarten, she learned the sounds of the letters she could already identify. She also began trying to put letters together to make words so she could record her thoughts on paper. She learned about rhyme and rhythm and chanted alliterative poems while experimenting with sounds and language.

Her teacher asked her to write daily in her journal in first grade. As she developed into a competent reader, her teacher also systematically shaped my daughter's writing and communication skills.

Although reading had not come overnight, by the end of first grade, reading was coming quickly, and she was delighted to read more books without adult help. This child read confidently and eagerly as she practiced reading at school and home.

By the end of the first grade, my child was reading with fluency and good expression with a mid-second-grade competency level. As a result of her success in reading, she was taking on many challenges from the extensive collection of books on her bedroom bookshelf. Her firm, beginning reading skills helped her have confidence and success as a reader.

Her sister, who started school one year later, was not as lucky. Although she had been read to and enjoyed listening to stories as much as her older sister, learning to decode the words on the page did not come as quickly for this child. Instead of learning to decipher the words on the page, she smiled and hid her confusion about the page's squiggles.

Being bright, she memorized the short, beginning reader passages. Since she could recite the words on the page quickly and fluently from memory, her teacher believed that she was making appropriate progress in learning to read. She mimicked the reading behaviors she saw her sister and other children doing in class. When she read at home, her reading was sporadic. She read the word, but two lines later, she could not decode the same word she had just read.

I started to suspect something was not going well but couldn't pinpoint the problem. Her teacher assured me that she was making appropriate progress in learning to read. She advised me not to worry.

By late first grade, the passages were getting too long to memorize. The fact that she was not on track with learning to read became apparent to my child's second-grade teacher, my husband, and me.

Unfortunately, my child did not have a highly skilled teacher who understood the reading process and how learning to read occurs. Her second-grade teacher was confused by her lack of progress in reading. It might have made a difference in her early reading development if she had been with a teacher with more reading skills.

My daughter received no differentiation, additional support, or special instruction at school. Her teacher continued to provide the same instruction despite knowing it was not working for my child. Her teacher was at a loss regarding how to help her and told us we should work more with her at home.

Since the second-grade teacher had failed my child and seemingly given up on her, I was determined to teach her to read. For this child, learning to read became a dreaded task requiring countless hours of practice and support. As any teacher who has tried to work with their own children knows, it is much easier to work with someone else's child than your own.

Over time and with practice and specific intervention, she did learn to read. We both did our best to make reading a fun and positive experience. Still, more often than not, our daily work time was filled with frustration and even a few tears on both of our parts along the way.

I am sorry to say that while she eventually learned to read, she never learned the joy of the printed page, nor how it feels to curl up with a beautiful book and lose oneself in the lives, problems, and struggles of various fictional characters.

My daughter is an adult with a family of her own now. She reads because it is necessary for her job and life—not because it brings her joy and fulfillment, as it does for me and her sister.

Had she had a more competent teacher, the support of a knowledgeable reading specialist at school, or had I known as much about how to help children learn to read, then maybe things would have been different for her. Unfortunately, that did not happen, and she has had to pay the price. Although that is water under the bridge, this is the reason that each child must be taught by a competent teacher.

Suppose there are problems and the reading skill does not come quickly or easily. In that case, the classroom teacher must know how to provide additional support for that child. The research about creating effective readers is much more detailed than during my children's school years.

We know from research what builds strong readers and writers; we must use this knowledge to help all children grow and prosper as readers. We must provide the best instruction and support possible so every child becomes a confident and capable reader.

As a reading coach, you hold the key to helping thousands of children and their teachers walk down this path and weave strong threads of foundational reading skills. Had my daughter's teacher had an effective reading coach to help her, perhaps she could have learned new ways to meet my daughter's instructional needs. Perhaps she could have learned to provide the targeted support my daughter so desperately needed when the instruction she was receiving was not helping her become a reader.

Unfortunately, there was no one to support this teacher. She didn't have a competent literacy coach to help her understand my daughter's needs and struggles. As a result of these failures, my daughter paid the price for her teacher's lack of skill in teaching reading.

Preparing Students in Grades 4-12 for the Changing Demands of the 21st Century

For students in grades 4-8, the purpose of education is to refine, deepen, and hone essential skills learned in elementary school. These skills include foundational reading, writing, math, problem-solving, and critical-thinking skills.

From grade 4, students work to expand and deepen their understanding of concepts and higher-order processing in subjects such as social studies, science, health, and literature. Teachers in grades 4-8 help students lay the groundwork for success in high school and help them make connections to the world around them and the content they are learning.

For decades, the purpose of high school has been to either prepare students for college or to prepare them with vocational skills that could be directly used in the workforce. With increased pressures from a globalized, highly competitive workforce from around the world now facing American workers, ensuring that American students can meet the most rigorous of standards in reading and writing has never been more critical.

We can no longer allow many students to drop out along the way or fail to thrive in our public-school systems. To continue to accept that some students will complete school without adequate reading, writing, and thinking skills is to doom these children to a life of poverty and a lifetime of struggle.

According to the U.S. Department of Labor website, at least one-third of the fastest-growing occupations projected to have the highest numerical increases in employment between 2021 and 2031 are in the healthcare industry. The next fastest-growing field is in professional, scientific, and technical services. The two fastest-growing major occupational groups consist of occupations that generally require postsecondary education or highly specialized training.

High-demand careers include nurses, physicians, communication and web designers, biomedical engineers, solar technicians, and medical scientists (Bureau of Labor Statistics, 2022).

The pressure to produce highly skilled, complex-thinking students has never been more significant in the history of American education. Unfortunately, high school reading scores have not improved significantly over the last thirty years and, in fact, have dropped by three points due to the impact of the COVID-19 pandemic (NAEP, 2022)

In light of the high standards and instructional demands placed on the high school today, high schools need literacy coaches more than ever before. With severe budget cuts nationwide, relatively few districts now provide this valuable support for their high school or middle school teachers, and this is not likely to change soon.

While high school teachers are outstanding in understanding their content areas, they have traditionally received little or no training to help students with reading skills. In addition, depending on where they were trained, some elementary teachers were not adequately prepared to teach elementary children to become strong readers.

Illiteracy in our country continues to grow. The US Department of Education found in a study with the National Institute of Literacy (2015) that approximately 32 million adults in the U.S. cannot read above a fifth-grade level. Additionally, over 8.7 million students in grades 4-12 cannot read and comprehend the textbook material. It is no wonder that poor reading skills, coupled with the impact of the COVID-19 pandemic, have caused high school dropout rates to rise in the United States (USA Facts, 2020) once again.

We must do our best to develop strong readers in the primary grades so that no child is left behind regarding successful reading and thinking. Since the 7-12 classroom is about applying and deepening conceptual knowledge, the classroom environment should have opportunities for directed learning, personal exploration, independent work, and peer collaboration.

Just as American factories have faded into the past, teacher-dominated classrooms with perfectly aligned rows of forward-facing seats that prepare students for factory work should also fade into the past. Today's classrooms should be vibrant, active, learner-centered places. Places where students of all ages are encouraged to explore their own interests, use technology, ask questions, and share their thoughts and ideas with peers regularly. Effective classrooms buzz with energy, collaboration, activity, curiosity, and the joy of sharing and exploring information.

Since teachers in grades 4-8 aim to help students learn to apply their foundational skills, make connections, and deepen conceptual understanding, effective literacy instruction must consider the context of our times and the needs of a high-tech, fast-paced, demanding world.

For students who get their reading exercise via the Internet, who tweet their daily thoughts, ideas, and actions, who communicate with friends via text instant messaging, and who record their personal histories on social networks such as Facebook and Tik Toc, the pace and relevance of many of our classrooms must be frustrating indeed. Promoting literacy as an isolated skill seems pointless in a world where many adults no longer read for pleasure. Instead, we must help students understand how to access, think, reason, and analyze the information surrounding them. Topping and McManus (2002) capture this perspective well:

> We can no longer assume that the Johnnys and Judys who come to us fully understand the "games" we want them to play. Therefore, we can no longer mete out only the sub-parts of the whole processes of reading, writing, listening, and speaking in any of our subjects, assuming that the students have in place the necessary skills and strategies for reading and writing in science, history, math, or health. We must not just tell but *show* our students what it is we want them to do, how we – the mature adults- read and write in our specific content areas, and then how we strategically control ideas and information within them. It's easy for educators to resent having to do this and to argue, that's not my job – I shouldn't have to – everyone else has abdicated. We understand this frustration. However, the job of real teachers is to *teach*, to do whatever is needed to get real students to learn. Our schools must reflect their culture and times, and we must change accordingly. (pgs. 13-14)

To do this, we must find authentic and practical ways to involve our students in meaningful experiences that allow them to authentically apply their learning.

We must let our students know our thinking processes by "thinking aloud" as we approach text, process text, and craft written tasks in our content area. We can model how to approach different reading and writing tasks in each discipline. Then we must show students how the work of math is different from the work of science or how expository text differs from narrative writing.

We must teach our students the appropriate strategies to approach and process various text types. We can help students understand that reading requires connecting what we already know to what we are reading. It also requires comparing and contrasting information and analyzing how it fits into our thinking and current paradigms.

Reading is not a passive act but a very active and engaging process. Successful readers actively construct meaning during the reading process. Without understanding, a reader is simply passing their eyes across the text.

We need to help students learn strategies to reflect on the text, such as comparing and contrasting information they find while reading. We can also show them how to analyze and sift out relevant and irrelevant details. Doing these things will prepare our students to transfer what they are learning to become literate readers.

Literacy Coaching—An Evolving Role

With pressure from states to increase student performance during the past decade, schools and districts have implemented instructional coaching programs to enhance and build teacher instructional skills, especially in critical areas such as reading.

According to research (Fullen & Hargreaves, 1992, 2007; Willis, Bland, Manka, & Croft, 2012), researchers have long understood the connection between collaborative school cultures and higher student achievement. Attempts to increase teacher collaboration positively correlate with improved teacher attitudes, enhanced teacher efficacy, long-lasting instructional changes, and higher student achievement.

Coaching and job-embedded professional development strategies are more effective ways of helping teachers to increase instructional effectiveness. Coaching, when properly implemented, can alter and deepen teacher practice (Darling-Hammond et al., 2009; Annenberg Foundation for Ed Reform, 2004). Researchers report that teachers are more likely to adopt new practices if they have also been coached (Knight, 2004; Neufeld & Roper, 2003; Showers & Joyce, 1996).

According to Rodgers and Pinnell, "Learners learn best by doing, and they learn faster if they have expert support as they try out new ideas" (2002, p. 1). Dozier (2006) states that teaching is about making connections, and learning is about moving beyond comfort zones. She states, "...at its best, literacy coaching is responsive, collegial, thoughtful, thought-provoking, deliberate, reflective, and transferrable" (p. 3). She says, "Rethinking instructional practices can be unnerving. It is far easier to ignore the complexities of learning and the attending uncomfortable moments that accompany being out of our safe zones." (p. 4).

Gallimore and Tharp (1990) state, "A teacher cannot provide assistance in the zone of proximal development (ZPD) unless she knows where the learner is in the developmental process" (p.198). Coaches must also make careful observations regarding the zones of proximal development of the teachers with whom they work.

This book is about rethinking instructional practices and moving out of our safe zones. It is about moving into the realm of the challenging, where we extend our personal and professional knowledge and expand our bag of tricks for the benefit of every student that crosses our threshold. Working side by side, coaches and teachers learn from one another and grow together, just as students and their teachers learn from one another and grow due to their contact and interaction.

The Historical Roots of Literacy Coaching

While many teachers might think that instructional coaching is a relatively new innovation, according to Bean and Wilson (1981), instructional coaching actually dates back to the 1930s. During this time, teachers who worked with other teachers to improve a school's reading program were first introduced to the school setting.

In the 1960s, Title 1 reading teachers who provided pull-out reading assistance to students were prevalent in high-poverty schools. In addition to providing direct services to students, some of these Title 1 reading teachers were also expected to be reading experts for the campus. These teachers were expected to provide demonstration lessons to their peers or to serve as reading resources to other teachers in their building.

By the 1980s and 1990s, Showers and Joyce (1996) report that more and more districts began using peer coaching to improve the implementation of new curricula and instructional techniques. According to their research, "teachers who had a coaching relationship—that is, who shared aspects of teaching, planned together, and pooled their experiences—practiced new skills and strategies more frequently and applied them more appropriately than did their counterparts who worked alone to expand their repertoires" (p. 14). The peer coach's role was well entrenched as a positive addition to district professional development efforts nationwide.

With the passage of NCLB in 2001 and the establishment of national K-3 Reading First grants in 2002, scores of districts were required to hire literacy coaches to work with classroom teachers. While these individuals were usually recruited from the ranks of successful master classroom teachers, many had little training on how to help teachers improve their practice in reading instruction.

In response to this dilemma, in 2004, the International Reading Association published a position statement entitled "The Role and Qualifications of the Reading Coach." This critical paper outlined the job role and established minimum qualification guidelines for professionals serving as literacy coaches.

The role of literacy coaching continued to evolve as coaches sought to define their role and make meaningful contributions to the teachers with whom they worked. The International Reading Association outlined five criteria that literacy coaches must possess. They were: be excellent classroom teachers and teachers of reading; be able to observe, model, and provide feedback to teachers; be knowledgeable about reading instructional practices; be excellent presenters; and, finally, be able to lead teacher groups to facilitate reflection and change.

In *Interactions: Collaboration Skills for School Professionals* (Friend & Cook, 2003), identify seven characteristics distinguishing adult learners from young learners. They say that coaches must understand these characteristics.

1. Adult students are mature people and prefer to be treated as adults. They learn best in a democratic, participatory, and collaborative environment. They need to be actively involved in determining how and what they learn and need active rather than passive learning experiences. They are self-reliant learners and prefer to work at their own pace.

2. Adults have needs that are concrete and immediate. They are task- or problem-centered rather than subject-centered. This doesn't mean they are not interested in a subject area. Still, their learning is incomplete until it is expressed in appropriate action. They tend to be impatient unless they see that information can be applied to practical problems.

3. Adults are more impatient in the pursuit of learning objectives. They are less tolerant of "busy work" that does not have immediate and direct application to their objectives. If it is irrelevant to their needs, they aren't very interested.

4. Adults have practical past experience. They are more realistic and have insights about what is likely to work and what is not. They are more readily able to relate new facts to past experiences and their background knowledge.

5. Adults enjoy using their talents and information in teaching. They bring their own experiences and knowledge into the classroom. They like the type of learning that gives them practical activities that build on their prior skills and knowledge.

6. Adults are intrinsically motivated. They are motivated by internal incentives and curiosity rather than by external rewards. They are also motivated by the usefulness of the material to be

learned and learn better when the material is related to their own needs and interests.

7. Adults are sometimes fatigued when they attend classes. They appreciate any teaching devices that add interest and a sense of liveliness, a variety of methods, audiovisual aids, a change of pace, and a sense of humor - anything that makes the learning process easier.

Russo (2004) reports that effective adult staff development must be "ongoing, deeply embedded in teachers' classroom work with children, specific to grade levels or academic content, and focused on research-based approaches. These characteristics should serve as a primary starting point to understand the needs, interests, and responses of teachers served in a coaching relationship. It also must help to open classroom doors and create more collaboration and sense of community among teachers in a school" (para.8).

There is ample evidence that intensive support, monitoring, and coaching levels help increase teacher instructional skills (Darling-Hammond & Richardson, 2009) and that professional conversations and ongoing dialogue among colleagues (Combs, 1994) increase teacher reflection. The purpose of professional development is to help teachers implement more effective practices. It is also to help teachers develop into strategic and reflective practitioners (Rodgers & Pinnell, 2002).

Over the last ten to fifteen years, many practical books have been written for instructional coaches on scheduling and structuring coaching time, establishing strong working relationships with teachers, and encouraging teachers to embrace change and expand their professional knowledge. Specific guidance for literacy coaches on examining instructional practices in the reading and writing content areas and helping teachers move from good to great in their instructional practices are also available for literacy coaches working with classroom teachers.

This book will delve into what good literacy instruction looks like in the day-to-day classroom by helping literacy coaches reflect on best practices in literacy instruction. More information on literacy instruction may be found in The *Threads of Reading: Strategies for Literacy Development* (Tankersley, 2003) and *Literacy Strategies for Grades 4-12: Reinforcing the Threads of Reading* (Tankersley, 2005). These books can be ordered from your favorite book retailer or from https://www.ascd.org. You can find additional information about the teaching of reading on my website https://threadsofreading.com.

Helping Teachers Improve Practice

Effective professional development is long-term and sustained through support and collaborative relationships. Most of the training is job-embedded work done in the classroom throughout the year. The classroom provides ample teacher practice, experimentation, inquiry, and reflection opportunities. Teachers can talk with their coach about what works and get help with questions or concerns as they try new skills and strategies.

The coach needs to be a person who is not only able to model effective literacy instruction but who can inspire and motivate colleagues to stretch and grow. Coaches cannot impose their own viewpoints or biases on their mentees. Still, they must help these teachers identify their interests, objectives, and milestones for success.

Literacy coaching is not an "improvement process" but a personal refinement process based on student learning for both teacher and coach. Literacy coaching expert Katherine Casey (2006) writes:

> ...the need for improvement shouldn't be seen as an attack or criticism but as a ray of hope as teachers strive to educate all students. If we believe it is our teaching, and not "teacher-proofed" curriculum materials or programs, that produces student learning, then improving our teaching to improve student learning is part of the act of teaching itself. The process must be embedded in our practice so that we reflect after each lesson on evidence of student learning to decide what students need next (pp. 23-23).

When coaches understand what outstanding reading instruction looks like, sounds like, and feels like at every level with which they work, they can genuinely help their peers "try on" the skills and techniques that enhance and weave strong foundational reading threads beneath and around the teachers and students with whom they work.

"...teaching isn't about teaching lessons. Teaching is about teaching students. Effective lessons aren't those that go according to plan. Effective lessons are lessons that are based on student needs, respond to student needs in the midst of their learning, and result in students' learning what they needed next."
Katherine Casey (2006, p. 165)

Chapter 1

Literacy Development for K-3 Teachers
The Productive Literacy Learning Environment
for K-3 Students

One of the first areas that a reading coach might want to help primary teachers examine is how the classroom environment supports developing readers. Primary students need a warm and accepting classroom where the teacher creates a bond of mutual love, respect, and patience with each child. The atmosphere is one of support, warmth, and encouragement, where various interesting experiences shape each day. Talking, singing, chanting, dancing, reading, play-acting, telling stories, drawing, and writing, all sprinkled with laughter and smiles, occur throughout the day. Children are encouraged to be risk-takers and to experiment and play with words, sounds, and print in fun and engaging ways. Errors are expected and considered an essential part of the learning process.

A productive literacy environment is where children are surrounded by print and submerged in it. Reading is clearly promoted from wall to wall. Students are surrounded by a plethora of words, letters, pictures, and books of every genre, size, and shape from the moment they enter the classroom. A productive literacy environment is identifiable even when no students are in the room because words, books, and enticing visuals abound. We can peek into three outstanding teachers' classrooms to learn more about what productive literacy environments at the K-3 level might look like.

What Does Reading Effective Instruction Look Like in Grades K-3?

Visiting Mary Jane – First Grade

The first teacher we will visit is Mary Jane. Mary Jane has taught first grade for twelve years and loves this age level. She has also taught third and kindergarten over the years but prefers the first grade since her great love is teaching students to get a good start in reading. As we peek into the classroom, it is apparent from the smiles and hugs that she and her twenty-eight students exchange that not only does Mary Jane loves her students, but they also love and are comfortable in her capable care.

Mary Jane's room has student desks organized in groups of four desks. Her small, well-organized teacher desk and chair are tucked back into a corner of the room, making it clear that Mary Jane does not spend much time there. In fact, it seems to function more as a materials-holding area than a workspace.

As we scan the walls, we see a word wall, a vocabulary area with words and pictures, and student drawings showing their favorite parts of *How I Became a Pirate* by Melinda Long and David Shannon. On the whiteboard, we can see evidence of a phonics lesson, and to the left of the whiteboard, a pocket chart with a letter-sound matching activity that has been recently used. Several poems, such as "Pop, Pop, Popcorn, Popping in the Pot," that have been written in marker on chart paper are posted on the wall. We assume the class uses these poems for phonemic awareness or chanting activities.

In another corner, we see a table with several copies of books by Mercer Mayer. Above the table, a colorful picture of the author is displayed. We also see several pictures of the covers of the author's books ringing the author's picture.

The table has a computer and a list of tasks that students can do independently. Each task is related to one of the Mercer Mayer books available in the center. Some puppets of Mercer Mayer characters, a box of writing and drawing paper, crayons, and colored pencils can also be found in the center.

Along the back wall is a small area labeled "writing center." There is a desk with paper and writing instruments such as pencils, pens, crayons, and colored pencils, along with paper for writing and drawing.

A sign above the area says "Reading Center." two large pillows are on the floor to the right of the writing center. A large tub is filled with colorful and appealing picture books. It sits between the 2 pillows.

To the left of this center is a large horseshoe table that Mary Jane uses for small-group guided reading. Behind the table on a countertop are small stacks of leveled books used during guided reading groups.

In the opposite corner is a large white, wicker rocker, where Mary Jane is seated. Next to the rocker is a smaller white wooden chair with the words "author's chair" painted across the top.

All the children are dutifully seated cross-legged on the colorful nursery rhyme rug in front of Mary Jane, eagerly listening to her read Bill Martin and Eric Carle's *Panda Bear, Panda Bear, What Do You See?*

Mary Jane uses a funny voice to differentiate the two speakers in the story. Her character's voices make the children laugh as she reads the story. The book sits on a book easel to her right. She uses a pointer so children can follow each word as she reads. Mary Jane knows this helps her students connect spoken words with their symbolic representation.

Mary Jane often stops to ask for predictions about what animal might be seen next in the book, and the children are eager to offer their opinions. She stops periodically and asks the children to identify a letter. Sometimes she asks them to decode a longer word after she says it slowly, phoneme by phoneme.
Mary Jane knows that this instructional technique helps students connect letters with sounds.

While reading, Mary Jane asks some children to repeat various words and asks others what sound they hear at the beginning of a specific word, such as "panda." She prompts when needed and suggests with a smile that children ask a neighbor when they need help answering her questions.

After listening to a page or two, one child tells Mary Jane that she has read a similar book called *Brown Bear, Brown Bear, What Do You See?* Mary Jane smiles and responds that this book is by the same authors. She says that she enjoys that book, too. She is pleased that the child noticed the pattern shared by the two books.

All students are eager to participate and follow along as Mary Jane reads. After a few pages of listening to the pattern, she asks the children to join in whenever she reads the "What do you see?" part. The children smile and join in eagerly.

Oral language activities and vocabulary work help her ELL students become more proficient in English. As she reads, she places a picture of each animal on a felt board on her left. Beneath the animal, she also places a card with the animal's name. She whispers to us that she has several English-language learners in the class, so she wants to ensure they have a visual cue to go along with the new vocabulary they are learning.

Soon the story is finished, and Mary Jane reminds students that several copies of the book are in the reading center for them to read to themselves this week. She lays the big book aside and asks the children to help her write a new story like the one they just read. She takes a marker and chart paper to jot down their ideas. The children are eager to offer their own story ideas using the pattern of the model story.

A special education aide enters the room. She quietly calls a group of six children to come to the horseshoe table. She begins working with her group on blending the sounds in specific words using Elkonin boxes.

Mary Jane smiles at us and nods as we quietly tiptoe out of the room and proceed down the hall to Jason's second-grade classroom.

Visiting Jason – Second Grade

Jason has been teaching second grade for five years. He taught fifth grade for three years before moving to second grade. Jason prefers working with younger students since he enjoys helping students develop into fluent readers.

There is an evident bond between students and teacher. While Jason is an effective reading teacher, science is his real passion. He loves to bring nonfiction books into the classroom whenever possible to compliment his science topics.

Jason's approach is more businesslike, but it is apparent that his students feel relaxed and safe in his room. Jason's classroom is arranged in groups of four desks pushed together. His teacher's desk, pushed tightly into a corner, looks more cluttered.
baskets of papers, files, and books are strewn across the desktop. Piles of papers look like they might topple to the floor at any moment.

Jason has an interactive whiteboard, a laptop, a document camera, and a projector in his classroom. The projector is placed where it can be used regularly for daily instruction. The interactive whiteboard appears to get a lot of use as well.

We see a word wall above the whiteboard with word cards from vocabulary that the children are learning. There is an attractive bulletin board labeled "Words We Love" with many words and corresponding pictures posted on them.

On another wall, there is a KWL chart. The chart displays information the students have generated about butterflies. On another wall are some samples of outstanding letters that students recently wrote to NASA telling them why they should have a visit from an astronaut for their school.

We see many scientific posters on the walls and science equipment on the shelves.

On a large bookcase, we see shelves full of books addressing the science topics students will be studying this school year. Stacks of magazines such as *Ranger Rick*, *Highlights*, and *National Geographic Kids* are also available for student use. Color-coded tubs of books are on the back counter.

Jason is seated at his horseshoe table, listening to a child read. He takes a running record of the child's reading performance, attentively marking the reading behaviors he hears on his running record sheet. He scans the room periodically to make sure the rest of the class is on task.

The other students are reading in pairs. Some are seated side by side in chairs. Others sit next to one another on the floor with their books shared across their laps. The children take turns reading a page, using low voices. Everyone is on task and focused on their reading. We can see that Jason's students frequently read as partners and are comfortable with the procedure.

As students come to a word they don't know, they look at a "strategy chart" Jason posted on the wall to figure out new words. They follow the steps listed on the chart to identify the new word.

Another sign on Jason's walls indicates, "Ask three before me." One group, who cannot figure out the word, quietly asks another pair of students for help with the word they don't know. After learning the meaning from their peers, they put a sticky arrow in the book pointing to the word they didn't recognize. Later, they will record the new word, write a definition using their own words, and draw a picture in their vocabulary notebooks. This practice will help them connect with the new vocabulary word in the future.

As Jason finishes the running record, he tells us that he has set a goal of listening to each child read at least twice a month to monitor their progress. He says using their performance data to flexibly group and regroup his students per their strengths and needs during guided reading time has helped their reading development. He points to the large stack of manila files on his desk.

Flexible grouping allows him to provide scaffolded instruction to guide them to the next step in their reading. This focused instruction, he says, has helped his students become more successful than they have been in the past. He apologizes for his students' soft "buzz" of oral reading. He says that giving each child more time to practice reading has helped improve the children's fluency.

A couple of groups finish their partner work early, pull out their iPads and silently read a story independently. Jason says that the students love reading on the iPads and that the school has lots of great books at the appropriate reading level for his students.

He reminds the students that if they have finished reading the story, they should now reread it with each partner taking the opposite page to read. He will work on word blending to identify unknown words with this group as they read. We thank him for his time as he waves and calls his lowest-level readers to work with him at the horseshoe table.

Visiting Megan – Third Grade

Our final visit is to Megan's third-grade class. Megan is a sixth-year teacher who loves reading, drawing, and writing stories in her spare time. She even considered becoming a librarian instead of a classroom teacher at one point in college. Megan has only taught third grade but loves working with this grade level. Her students enjoy her "artsy" and quirky love of reading. Megan is a good artist, and her room is filled with many books, magazines, and other reading materials, but also colorful drawings of some of the characters from the stories she shared with the class.

Megan also has a word wall and a bulletin board with the words "What's so Phunny?" in the center. Students record their favorite puns and jokes on index cards and attach them to this bulletin board. Megan says that her third-grade students roll with laughter when she reminds them that "ph" says /f/, and they realize that the bulletin board's title is "What's so funny?"

Megan had the desks that used to be in her classroom replaced with round tables. Her neatly organized teacher's desk is tucked away in the upper front corner of the room. At the back of the room is a free-standing "cubby" area where students keep their books and materials. Each cubby is labeled with one student's name in decorative script.

Megan smiles and greets us at the door as we arrive at her classroom. She says today is a discussion day, so we can listen to student discussions. She tells us that her students participate in bi-weekly literature circles. Each group has chosen their own book to read and discuss.

On each table is an empty book basket. Students use their books to search for and cite examples that support their ideas and conclusions as they discuss their books.

Children all wear a tag tied with bright yarn that announces their discussion role in their literature group. Roles include Discussion Leader, Fact Checker, Word Wizard, and Connector. We note that various groups are discussing novels of several levels.

Students appear to be interested and involved in lively discussions about their books all around the room. Megan explains that students are given time to read once per week in class. If they do not complete the assigned portion of the text, they take the book home to finish it at home. The next day, they discuss what they have read.

Literature groups are just a tiny part of her weekly literacy-building routine. During the remaining days of the week, she works with flexible, guided reading and independent reading groups, just as Jason does with his students.

Megan has been using literature circles for three years after attending a three-week summer workshop on this technique. She thinks the students have greatly benefited from reading trade books matching their reading levels and interests.

Over the three years, she has perfected an approach that works for her and her students. The students appear to understand their roles and confidently discuss and challenge one another's thinking about the material they have read.

As we watch, one group member disagrees with a statement made by another group member. He politely asks the group Fact Checker to find the page and paragraph in the text that discusses the matter so the argument can be resolved. All students begin flipping pages, eager to find the part in the text that will answer the dispute.

Megan flits around the room, takes a chair, and listens to various group discussions. She does not participate but notes how the students reason and express themselves during the discussion. While each group reads a different book matching their reading level, Megan tells us that all the books support a theme she calls "Making Friends."

When the discussion begins to wane, Megan calls the class to order. She asks students to discuss how the characters in their books were making friends, getting along, or having problems in their friendships. Megan asks them to think about how the characters might have handled things differently and, if they had, what outcomes might have evolved. Students offer some examples from their books.

Megan reminds students that by reading, we can see how other people got into problems and then were able to solve their problems. This can help us become better problem solvers when situations happen to us in our own lives. She then asks students to discuss how their own experiences have been similar to or different from those of the characters in their books. The students agree.

As students wrap up the discussion, Megan reminds them to silently read their guided reading story for homework. She tells them to put sticky flags near any new words they do not know. She tells the class she looks forward to hearing their comments about the story and having them work on a class readers' theater that she has found with another version of the same story. The students' faces brighten at the mention of the readers' theater, and students are clearly happy about tomorrow's activity.

As the class prepares for lunch, we tiptoe out of the classroom to reflect on what we have seen in the three classrooms we have observed.

Best Literacy Practices for Grades K-3

Since all three of these classrooms were doing very different things as we peeked in on them, you may wonder which techniques were "best practices" in literacy instruction. The truth is that all of these teachers were using best practices, even though they were using very different strategies.

I once heard someone ask reading expert Pat Cunningham to list what she felt were the best instructional strategies that a teacher could use. Pat's reply was, "For which child?" She explained that since every child is unique, teachers must know many ways to teach literacy skills. As she said, what works for one child might not be the right strategy for another.

Since K-3 students have many needs, effective literacy instruction for K-3 students has many components. By carefully observing and changing our instructional approaches to meet each child's needs, we can provide appropriate instructional support to help all K-3 children become successful readers, writers, and thinkers.

As we observed our three teachers, we found warm and safe environments where students collaborated with one another. There was mutual affection and respect, and students enjoyed participating in each classroom. It was also clear that student needs and interests were the focal points of the teacher's planning and instruction.

Although the teacher styles differed, and we witnessed only a small snippet of daily literacy instruction, common threads of effective literacy instruction ran through each classroom. Let's explore some of these commonalities.

At the first-grade level, our teacher deliberately planned activities that strengthened her children's phonemic awareness and expanded their vocabulary. She knew that the two most critical skills for beginning readers are their level of phonemic awareness and their knowledge of letters and sounds. She understood that these are the two best predictors of how well children will learn to read during their first two years of formal reading instruction (National Reading Panel Report from the National Institute of Child Health and Human Development, 2000).

She used predictable books rich with opportunities to link letter and sound identification, phonemic awareness, and phonics. She also used controlled vocabulary books to help students master the sounds and symbols they need to become effective readers.

She helped all of her students visualize elements of story and character. She used graphic organizers, realia, and expanded vocabulary opportunities to support ELL learners in her classroom.

The classroom had a rich supply of charts and easels with large pads of paper available. An adequate supply of writing materials, such as chart paper, writing paper, markers, crayons, stamps and stamp pads, journal notebooks, and child-friendly tape recorders with microphones, were also available for student use. The teacher and students used these resources to craft messages, read poems, or sing songs written on the chart paper's pages.

Word-rich, interactive bulletin boards, word walls, big books, and book displays grabbed students' interest and encouraged students to examine the materials in greater detail. Word walls, collections of new vocabulary, and evidence of playing with words were apparent.

The class had soft furniture for cozying up to read or discuss books. A rug or classroom author's chair beckoned students to surround the teacher or guest reader to hear the latest story being read aloud.

In grades two and three, we saw students being encouraged to practice reading, expand their vocabularies, and learn to derive meaning from text.

We saw ample use of fiction and nonfiction, the use of controlled vocabulary, and the use of authentic text. We also saw the linkage of nonfiction text to content area instruction. Authentic writing tasks helped students connect their thoughts and ideas to purposeful action.

We saw classrooms that fostered student independence and collaboration yet provided scaffolded support to help students who needed more individualized support. Assessment, observation-guided instruction, and flexible, ever-changing grouping strategies helped students receive "just right" instruction. These strategies helped expand word knowledge and build effective reading skills for K-3 students.

Providing Support for Teachers in Grades K-3

First, let's consider the classroom learning environment. We know children learn best in a positive, stress-free environment that encourages risk-taking and curiosity. Effective K-3 classrooms where strong literacy skills are developed generally exhibit a warm, open, and inviting climate where children can take risks and use their natural curiosity.

The reading coach can use a list of questions to help the K-3 teachers reflect and select areas to target for growth and development. Consider the following characteristics as you think about each K-3 classroom environment:

- •Does the classroom have a warm, open, and inviting feeling when you enter the room, and do students clearly enjoy being in the classroom?
- •Does the teacher clearly love reading and model enjoyment of reading themselves?
- •Does a high amount of talk occur in the classroom throughout the day from the teacher and among children? Do children enjoy talking and interacting with their teacher and one another?

• Do students regularly work together in fluid pairs, triads, or small groups?
• Is there an abundance of easily accessible, age-appropriate fiction and nonfiction books in the classroom? Does the classroom contain other print elements such as magazines, newspapers, labels, catalogs, signs, charts, and word-rich bulletin boards?
• Are there charts with lists, recipes, songs, poems, communications, etc., around the room where children can read and work with them?
• Are print and images representative of the cultures and races of student populations readily visible in the classroom?
• Do both students and teacher display their natural curiosity during the day? Are students and teachers smiling most of the time, and do they appear to enjoy what they are doing?

Questions to analyze the literacy instruction taking place in the classroom:

• Does the teacher prepare students for reading by activating student background knowledge before reading? Are concepts clarified with examples and/or illustrations so children can link concepts to a familiar frame of reference?
• Are children frequently encouraged to observe, ask questions, and link their background knowledge to new learning? Does the teacher link new concepts with examples or illustrations (both visual and verbal) regularly?
• Does the teacher use many genres of reading in the classroom and often repeat student favorites regularly?

- Does the teacher encourage children to read and write throughout the school day? Are there opportunities for authentic and purposeful reading and writing?

- Does the teacher use anticipatory questions or picture walks to introduce new books, and do they ask students to regularly make predictions before and during reading?

- Does the K-1 teacher use read-aloud time to instruct students on the concepts of print, such as directionality, handling of books, and various text elements such as title, author, illustrator, etc.? Does the 1st- to 3rd-grade teacher use read-aloud time to discuss concepts such as author, illustrator, title page, and story elements?

- Does the teacher use shared reading to reinforce reading skills and flexibly group and regroup students regularly according to instructional needs?

- Does the teacher use appropriate technology to promote student interest and excitement in reading?

- Does the teacher use appropriate assessments and regular observations to guide student needs, guided reading work, and flexible grouping practices?

- Do struggling readers have additional support within the classroom to help them close the gap between their current performance level and grade-level expectations? [Does the school have Tier 2 and Tier 3 RtI support for those who need more intensive help? Does the teacher use these supports to ensure early literacy success?]

In addition to these broad questions, you will want to help the teacher analyze instruction in phonemic awareness and phonics, fluency and vocabulary development, comprehension and higher-order reading, and connecting writing to reading.

The charts in the resources section can help you and the teacher analyze teacher performance in each area. These areas can also serve as the basis for collaborative goal-setting. Provide the survey to each teacher you work with and encourage them to complete the self-evaluation privately.

Ask them to write down two or three areas where they want coaching assistance in the next few months. Together, you will write these into S.M.A.R.T. goals to be mutually worked on during the next few weeks. Putting these into written goals will help you focus everyone's attention on what you are trying to improve and help you better track each teacher's professional development plans. Make sure that your goals are observable and measurable so that you can easily measure and assess progress.

If you are a veteran coach who has already built a strong, trusting relationship with the group of teachers with whom you work, you may be able to help guide the discussion about the teacher's current strengths and areas for growth.

If this is a new coach-coachee relationship, let the teacher select the most relevant goals without attempting to influence them. Remember that adult learners not only want to direct their own learning, but they also want to be able to directly apply those skills to make a difference with their students.

Initially, some teachers may choose topics they already feel comfortable with, particularly those who may be less self-assured with their reading instruction. This enables them to reduce their own risk in the situation. This may happen if they have not established a rapport and trust with you as their coach. Allow this for now as you work to build a trusting relationship with your coachee.

Building a collegial relationship and establishing trust and mutual respect are more important at the beginning of your work with each teacher. With time and a strong, positive relationship, the adults with whom you work will place more and more trust in you and reveal more areas where they need help and support. No matter what they choose to focus on, accept their choices even if you disagree with the teacher's self-assessment.

As you visit and work with other primary teachers on your campus, note some strategies and methods that seem to work well. You can then share these tips and ideas with other teachers. If you see an effective teacher who has mastered the skills that one of your teachers would like to learn, consider offering to take the teacher's classroom, so they can spend time observing the "pro" at work.

As you observe the teacher's instruction and develop a strong relationship with that individual, you can suggest ways to continue to build a more positive literacy experience for students.

Building Literacy in the Primary Classroom

For many classroom teachers, the techniques described in this section may be "old hat," while to others, they may be relatively new ideas that need to be learned.

Just as we saw when we "peeked" into the three teacher classrooms, the various instructional approaches may vary by grade level or student need, but, nonetheless, all of these elements should be part of the primary teacher's instructional "bag of tricks" to provide strong and comprehensive reading instruction to primary students.

Full descriptions of each element have been provided here to ensure we use the same terms to refer to the same instructional strategies. These descriptions may also help you describe or clarify elements for teachers who need to learn these instructional strategies.

Teacher Read-Alouds

Reading aloud is a daily necessity for all K-3 classrooms. Most experienced primary teachers understand the importance of reading aloud to their students and regularly incorporate a daily read-aloud book into their schedule. Read-alouds can help students enhance their vocabulary, learn new ideas and concepts, develop an interest in and love for reading, and understand new perspectives or ways of viewing the world.

Read-aloud time is a good place for teachers to model oral expression, curiosity, and their love of books and their characters. Reading books together builds a positive and fun connection to texts of all types. It also allows older children to access material they are not yet ready to read independently.

When you ask adults to describe their most positive memory about their time in school, most adults often cite being read to by their teacher as the most memorable experience from their school years. Reading regularly introduces children to the characteristics of books, expands vocabulary, builds background knowledge, and teaches children how to handle text. Listening to stories helps children lengthen their attention span, anticipate sequence, and make and test predictions.

Being read to can uncover new ways of thinking and looking at the world or provide them with viewpoints and experiences that they might not otherwise have had. Read-alouds also create an atmosphere of fun and help children associate pleasure with reading.

Reading aloud can not only help students notice and enjoy the lilt and playfulness of language, but it can also strengthen oral language, enhance listening skills, and strengthen phonemic development. This is especially true for children from impoverished backgrounds or those with English as a second language. Even in a half-day kindergarten program where time is at a premium, scheduling time to read aloud to students, even for a few minutes, is one of the highest and best uses of time to build strong literacy skills.

To strengthen their background knowledge, teachers must help their students build connections with ideas and concepts that the students already know. Using nonfiction for read-alouds can help expose children to new concepts and enhance their understanding of concepts and factual information.

For English language learners or children from impoverished homes, this background knowledge building can better prepare children for content learning and for closing the achievement gap between impoverished children and their more affluent peers who already have this information when they enter school.

Repetition of favorite stories and being able to "read" a story from memory are essential understandings for primary children. Mimicking adult reading helps children make the connection that reading is just "talk written down." In fact, "pretend reading" is an important foundational stage in connecting with print for young children.

Every parent who reads to their child quickly learns that children will request the same favorite books time after time. They also learn that even before the child can decode the symbols on the page, young children who are frequently read to are proficient at memorizing and "reading" the lines of their favorite stories.

This is a natural progression in literacy development that helps motivate young children to actually learn to decode the words in their favorite books on their own.

Classroom read-aloud time is often done with the teacher (or guest reader) seated in a special chair, like a rocking chair or bean bag chair, in a designated part of the room. Primary children are seated on the floor at the reader's feet on the carpet or individual rugs. This makes reading time "cozier" and more personal for children, similar to the experience of reading on a parent's lap.

Some kindergarten teachers may even have children stretch out on their own rugs to rest during the listening time to help relax them. Big books are often used for read-aloud sessions so children can easily see the pictures.

Sometimes normal-sized books are read, but the teacher makes sure to share the pictures with the group after the page has been read. During read-aloud time, the teacher can foster enjoyment of the book and help children learn about the concepts of print, such as left-to-right and top-to-bottom progression, the concepts of author, illustrator, title page, and similar concepts.

Some skills that might be taught are that books have pages that are turned to continue the story; they have orientation, with a right way and a wrong way to hold them and progress through them. They should also learn that the pictures help tell the story; that text is read with attention to directionality; and, finally, that books are a source of interesting information, enjoyment, and fun.

Read-alouds are a good time for the teacher to share concepts with young children about a text, such as "author," "illustrator," "title," "illustrations," "table of contents," and so forth. Children learn that books can be silly or sad, true or purely made up.

As children learn to connect text to themselves, their world, and other texts, they learn that text can remind us of things that happen in our lives and help us understand what happens in our world. We learn to value books by listening to them read by enthusiastic adults who clearly model their enjoyment of books and their content.

Before beginning a read-aloud, take a minute to activate children's prior knowledge by getting students to talk about "what they know" about the book's topic before they hear it read aloud. This discussion can help determine students' connections to the topic. Ask students to make predictions about the book based on the cover photo or artwork of the book or the title of the book if this lends itself to insightful discussion.

Walk through the pictures in the book with your fingers and ask students to predict what they think the book will be about or what might happen in the book. Use read-aloud time to expose children to various genres and help them learn that books come in many shapes and sizes and on different topics.

Books should also help students connect to their own backgrounds and cultural foundations. Choose books reflecting students' cultural backgrounds, and use a good blend of fiction and nonfiction for daily read-aloud time. Whenever possible, connect relevant fiction and nonfiction text to other content areas, such as math, science, or social studies. The more children are exposed to text throughout their day, the better.

Before reading any text to students, spend a few minutes activating the students' prior knowledge of the subject. When students make connections before reading a text, they enhance their ability to make sense of it and connect it to what they already know. When you read, use high vocal drama, even over-exaggeration, to help children connect with the story.

When using text with dialogue, use funny voices, exaggerated expressions, or volume and pitch changes to tell the story. This helps children have fun, identify the speakers, and connect more with the story. Puppets can also "read" the story if the teacher is shy about "hamming it up" with children.

Be sure to incorporate a good quantity of books with conversation so that children can clearly see that books are "talk written down." As the words are read, pointing to and saying them will help young children learn to read, track print correctly, and connect words with the symbols on the page.

Stop periodically to analyze predictions, clarify vocabulary as needed, or ask "who, what, why, when, where, and how" questions. Teachers might also ask open-ended, reflective questions like: "Did it surprise you when…?" or "Do you think…?" or "What did you enjoy about the story?" or "How were the characters like you?" or "What did this story make you think about?"

Whenever possible, help students reflect on the deeper meaning and think about higher-level questions or issues that the book presents. Helping students go deeper into the text helps them connect with the text in more meaningful ways. It also helps children think about ideas and issues more deeply and relate their reading to their lives.

Ask students to visualize scenes or characters from the books shared during read-aloud time by describing the "movie scene" they see in their minds. Young children can further reinforce these visualizations by drawing favorite scenes or specific characters from the book. Children can also act out parts of the book, taking on the roles of their favorite characters. This visualization helps develop imagination and clarify understandings.

As you read, stop on challenging or new words to discuss them. You can also show a picture or an example, provide a synonym, or help children connect with the new word. Children must link a concept they already know with the new word to add it to their accessible vocabulary. After the read-aloud session, add a few new words to a word wall and help students find a pictorial way to link the new words to their existing knowledge. Practice the more common new words daily until the words become easily accessible to the children.

There is no better way to expand vocabulary and create a love for books than by reading aloud to children throughout their school careers. Read-aloud time should continue on a daily basis for at least 10-20 minutes throughout the primary grades.

Sometimes teachers do not read aloud to their students because they have limited time (such as in a half-day kindergarten program) or think it takes too much time out of their day. For teachers who are not sure about the time required for incorporating daily read-alouds, assure them that reading aloud is not only one of the best ways to enhance and build vocabulary, it is also a great way to increase conceptual development, expose students to new ideas, and foster student interest in learning to read.

Since listening abilities develop ahead of reading abilities, read-alouds allow students to enrich their understanding and access material that might be beyond their reading abilities. This is especially important for high-poverty children or children from multicultural backgrounds where English is not the first language.

Oral Language Building

As K-1 children play with words and notice rhyme and rhythm, their oral language skills are enhanced. Loban (1976) observed that children with strong oral language skills in kindergarten later became the most proficient readers and writers. For this reason, oral language experiences must play a significant role in every child's classroom experience during the kindergarten and 1st-grade years. Oral language should be interspersed throughout the day at planned times and when extra transition minutes are needed during the school day.

Learning to talk is genetically hard-wired. Children learn to speak by listening to those around them speak and by responding back to others. Oral language experiences include verbal games, choral poetry reading, singing songs, and participating in word play activities that promote letter and sound recognition, rhyme, and vocabulary development. The higher the percentage of low-income or non-English-speaking students in the classroom, the more essential it is that oral language be a focus of classroom literacy efforts.

Despite the benefits of learning by imitation, linguists also know that children develop linguistic rules independently. For example, a child might say, "I gived it to him" or "I seed him" while trying to sort through irregular past tense verbs. As the child's language skills grow, they will learn to use the proper tense and change the statement to "I gave it to him." This happens naturally for most children as they continue to be exposed to language patterns. Learning to talk, like learning to walk, takes time, exposure, and practice. The better the children's language skills, the more quickly they learn to read and write.

The semantic component of language consists of morphemes, the smallest units of language. We use our background knowledge and experiences to determine what makes sense when we hear words and phrases. The final component, the syntactic component, helps us combine words into phrases and sentences.

When children first learn to express their wants and desires, it may be in simple word combinations such as, "Go bye-bye" or

"Gimme drink." As the child matures, he learns to add prefixes and suffixes, use inflectional endings, and even use irregular tense constructions. The child eventually creates questions, statements, commands, or demands as they learn to manipulate their mother tongue.

As children mature, they also understand pragmatic aspects of language, which help us determine how to speak appropriately in different situations and with different people. Teachers must model good conversational skills, such as taking turns when speaking, looking attentively at the speaker, using appropriate facial expressions, and so forth so that children continue to understand the pragmatic rules of conversation.

Activities that encourage interaction between children, such as dramatic play, readers' theater, book sharing, and shared writing, are just a few ways teachers can help reinforce and build solid oral language skills. Strong oral language skills enhance every curriculum area, so the K-1 classroom should be alive with talk and oral language.

We know that all good readers use three cueing systems to make meaning of language: the phonological, the semantic, and the syntactic (Lindfors, 1987). Children develop their sense of syntax and semantic meaning by attending to the patterns of oral language they hear. The phonological component is the "rules" we learn to follow for combining sounds in English. For example, we learn that the letters "qu" can occur at the beginning of a word but not at the end or that the suffix "-ing" can occur at the end but does not occur at the beginning of an English word.

While these are not conscious rules that someone has taught us, all of us, no matter what language we are learning to speak, come to understand at a very early age where sounds commonly occur in our mother language and how sounds are combined in our language. By the time children start formal schooling, children know the phonological fundamentals of their native language. They can use the most common structures and patterns with reasonable accuracy.

At the K-1 level, the keys to oral language development are frequent contact with sounds, syllables, and rhyme concepts. Children transition into developing an awareness of how words are put together by playing with these parts of words. They also learn that words make up the "talk" they hear around them.

There is a clear reason why Mother Goose rhymes were mothers' favorite for generations. They work well to build strong foundational reading skills. Singing songs, doing finger plays, and listening to rhythmic poetry enhances oral language development and builds oral language skills. From these understandings, it is much easier to understand that words are organized into sentences communicating our thoughts, feelings, and ideas.

You can help K-1 classroom teachers self-reflect on the amount of oral language development in the classroom. The higher the percentage of non-English-language learners or high-poverty students in the classroom, the higher the percentage of oral language activities needed. Help teachers identify additional ways to expand oral language use so that children have many opportunities to hear oral language and practice it continually.

Shared Oral Reading Time

While the teacher may use this time to model concepts of print and learn about authors, illustrators, and the parts of a book, the time is primarily spent in grades K-1 reading the story to uncover the letter-sound relationships contained in the text. While children should still enjoy listening to the story, the goal of this time is not just to listen to interesting stories and talk about them; the primary focus of shared oral reading is to enhance phonemic awareness and learn more about the phonological patterns of language.

During shared reading, children explore sounds, letters, words, and sentences in more detail and how they work together to form meaning in the text. Time is spent helping students expand their understanding of letter-sound relationships, segmenting, blending, and identifying elements such as words; sentences; initial, final, and medial sounds; and other elements related to phonemic awareness and the understanding of print. During shared reading time, the teacher may use a "big book" or other enlarged text to read a story, just as they did during read-aloud time. Still, this time the book selection is based on specific skills that the teacher wants to emphasize.

Strong phonological awareness distinguishes good readers from poor readers. To increase letter knowledge and the ability to distinguish and identify the letters of the alphabet, teachers can use poetry or songs that are alliterative or have an abundance of rhyme to strengthen children's phonemic awareness skills. Rhymes and finger plays can also build sound-symbol awareness and help children learn the "lilt" of the English language. In addition to working with text to strengthen students' phonological awareness, opportunities to identify objects in the classroom whose names begin or end with the same sound as a given sound being emphasized in the text can also help sharpen phonemic awareness skills.

Repetitive pattern books, books with rhyme, or books that emphasize a specific phonological pattern should be used during shared reading time. For example, when working with the initial sound of the letter *m* with students, the teacher might choose *The*

Misadventures of Minnie Mouse since the book contains ample use of the initial /m/ sound. The teacher calls the children's attention to the /m/ sound as they read through the book's text and asks them to make the sound and identify it as they hear the teacher read the story. Teachers can also have students "guess" the rest of the word by covering certain parts of the word with "sticky notes." This is especially useful with predictable books or books with clearly identified rhyme patterns.

Coaches can model for teachers how to select a book where certain letters, sounds, or words can be covered with "sticky notes" and uncovered as students identify what letters are "hiding" under the sticky note. As you work through the book with students, help them focus on strengthening their letter-sound understandings.

Books can be selected to reinforce concepts such as ending sounds, medial sounds, compound words, and so forth as the need arises. Once teachers see this modeled a couple of times, you might assist them in selecting their own books that coordinate with the letters or sound patterns they want to teach. Learning to reinforce student phonemic understanding in this way is an excellent way to build and reinforce letter-sound relationships.

In addition to reinforcing letters, words, and sounds, teachers can use shared reading time to reinforce letter recognition and help students understand and note punctuation in text. Another effective method of helping students identify certain sounds is to have them raise their hands or stand when certain letters, sounds, or rhyme patterns are heard. This is especially helpful for students when reading books that contain dialogue in the text. Again, model with classroom teachers how to help students notice and identify key sounds they hear as the text is read or pay attention to punctuation in the text.

Children can also sharpen their skills at predicting phonemic sequence by guessing rhyming pattern words that fit the context. Children love to read and re-read pattern books, so it is always a good idea to place copies of pattern books in a center area after they have been read aloud in class.

When these books are available in centers, children can spend time reading and re-reading their favorite pattern books with one another. Providing paint stir sticks to use as text pointers can also be fun. This will encourage children to take turns acting as the teacher, reading the book to the other children in the center area. Big books can also be placed in centers by staging them on an easel and allowing children to "play teacher" for a small group of friends or classmates.

As children progress in decoding and recognizing letter-sound relationships, teachers should also ensure that the books they choose can build sight vocabulary and help children with sequencing, making predictions, making inferences and drawing conclusions, and connecting events found in the book with their own background knowledge and experiences. The teacher might help students remember the sequence of significant events in the book or recall some vital information by creating a few lines on chart paper with blank spaces for the appropriate response. For example, the teacher might write on chart paper: "First, Jerry went to buy a _____. Then he went to _____. Finally, he went _____." or "Flowers need _____ and _____ to grow."

Since summarization is one of the most powerful learning skills that students can master (Marzano, Pickering, & Pollack, 2001), teachers should help students learn to summarize the books that they are reading, even as early as 1st grade. Students can recall the book's information and help fill in the missing details orally. At the same time, the teacher records their answers in the appropriate blanks.

For students in grades two and three, shared reading is when the teacher explicitly teaches a reading strategy through modeling and think-alouds. Students then apply the new strategy individually as they read orally in a small guided reading group or in paired reading groups where students take turns reading. Shared reading is *not* round-robin reading, where the whole class takes a turn reading the text. According to research, this strategy is the least effective of all reading instructional strategies at building competent and confident readers (Opitz and Rasinski, 1998).

Shared reading should be done in conjunction with the daily lesson. It should introduce or reinforce the skills the teacher is trying to develop in students. It is a way to link students' learning to what they need next and help them refine their understanding along the way. It is the practical application of skills to authentic reading tasks that help children refine their understandings and link them to text.

Guided Reading

Guided reading is practice reading done by the student with closely monitored assistance from an adult. The purpose of guided reading is to help primary students become more proficient and automatic decoders of text independently.

Guided reading (which should occur daily for fifteen to twenty minutes for every student) is generally done with smaller, more homogeneous groups of readers reading at similar reading proficiency levels. During this time, the teacher can gain important information about how each child is progressing and determine the next steps for instruction. Students work with the teacher or a classroom assistant (adult aide, parent volunteer, or older student) on an appropriately leveled book or with a controlled text at their instructional level. The adult listens to the children as they read orally, provides feedback, and asks questions about the comprehension of the material as children read.

The facilitator may also provide short mini-lessons related to new vocabulary or demonstrate specific reading strategies that may be appropriate for the material being read or for the student's stage of reading development. Children in the class who are not engaged in the guided reading group may be reading independently or working in technology or in reading learning centers.

The first step in establishing well-functioning guided reading groups is to use assessment data, such as the information gained from running records or other assessments, to place students into groups of readers with similar instructional needs. Groups should be fluid so students are grouped and regrouped according to development and skill need.

The teacher selects a text within the students' control but pushes their skills slightly. The teacher introduces the text, clarifies any unusual vocabulary that may be needed, and provides some connective information on the text. The teacher then helps students reflect on and bring out their own understandings and connections relative to the topic of the material.

Students then read the selected text silently or to the small group in a soft voice while the teacher listens and assists as needed. After reading, the teacher interacts with children about the text to clarify understanding, assist in recalling or sequencing events, provide strategies that may be needed, or clarify any other needed aspects of the reading process. The discussion helps clarify understanding and allows students to express their ideas, connections, and inferences about the material they read. The teacher should jot down notes and observations about each reader while they are fresh in their mind.

As a result of observing readers during the guided reading process, the teacher will most likely observe the need for specific instruction in specific processes or strategies to help students take their reading to the next level. Instruction is then provided to the guided reading group or, occasionally, the whole class in a "mini-lesson" on the topic students need to learn. This scaffolded instruction allows students to reach for the subsequent understanding without being overwhelmed by material or challenging skills. This gentle support will allow children to grow and develop as readers.

The mini-lesson is short and specific and is designed to help students refine their skills and advance performance and understanding to the next level. For example, the teacher might demonstrate a reading process, such as asking questions during reading to aid comprehension, and then ask students to practice this strategy during guided reading.

Another example is that the teacher might explain and model a strategy, such as re-reading a sentence when meaning is lost to regain comprehension of the material. Other topics that might be explained and practiced during a mini-lesson include a new decoding strategy, exploring a specific language construction, a phonics concept for attacking new words with a similar word pattern, or a spelling principle to identify common spelling patterns that might occur in certain groups of words.

Following the mini-lesson, students directly apply the skills they have learned to print during the guided reading experience. During this time, teachers can provide extensive support to ensure the skills or concepts are correctly applied while reading.

Strengthening Phonemic Awareness Skills

Researchers tell us that a child's phonemic awareness level by the end of first grade can account for as much as fifty percent of the variance between weak and proficient beginning readers (Blackman, 1991, Juel, 1991, Snow, Burns & Griffin, 1998).

We also know that children who fall behind in first grade will have only a one in eight chance of ever catching up to their grade-level peers (Juel, 1994). For this reason, it is absolutely essential that teachers understand the importance of foundational phonemic awareness skills and that they have the tools to help students fully develop their foundational reading skills before leaving first grade.

In addition to experiencing the types of reading, writing, and oral language activities we discussed in the previous sections, teachers should regularly help students take apart and experiment with the various sounds that make up the English language. Phonemic awareness skills are the bedrock foundation upon which effective reading skills are built for early primary students. The most crucial phonemic awareness skills critical to foundational reading are letter identity recognition, phoneme isolation, segmenting, and blending words.

Since word recognition is directly tied to a student's ability to blend the individual sounds they see into a word the child recognizes, blending phonemes into recognizable words is perhaps the most essential skill students need. Too often, teachers move too quickly over this crucial area before students have become proficient at blending words. Helping them make sure that their students can blend phonemes into intelligible words they can recognize is critical. Strong blending skills will significantly impact a student's reading success.

Effective phonemic awareness instruction teaches children to notice, think about, and manipulate the sounds in spoken language. The English language has approximately forty-four phonemes that students must know and be able to manipulate (Blevins, 1998). At the K-1 level, teachers must work to develop phonological awareness skills moving from simple to complex (Kruidenier, 2002).

During oral phonemic awareness activities, students practice recognizing and producing words that rhyme and words that don't rhyme. Students should also be taught to identify words that have alliterative sounds.

Primary teachers should also develop the concept of syllables and words in early primary readers. One of the ways to do this is by asking children to identify "How many syllables do you hear in the word 'baby.'"

Once children can recognize the syllables in a word, they should then be taught to recognize the concept of a word. They should also understand that words are placed into sentences. To help students understand the concept that words make up sentences, teachers can ask students to determine how many words are in various sentences. The teacher might ask, "How many words are in the sentence, 'I see my mother?'"

As children continue examining speech patterns, they should manipulate the onset and rime sounds they hear in a word. For example, children can use the rime pattern "ot" to make new words they recognize. For example, the word "hot" can become "pot," "not," "cot," "rot," "tot," and so forth.

Researchers note that adults read by noting the rime families of words as they quickly pass over text while reading. Helping children understand how initial consonants change the word's meaning can help them note this relationship. Activities in phoneme identity, isolation, deletion, and practice blending letters and syllables will form the basis for developing solid phonemic awareness. The areas of instruction in phonemic awareness are:

- •Understanding the concepts of print (how to hold a book, track left to right, track top to bottom, etc.).
- •Recognizing and using rhyme and alliteration and building sound awareness
- •building an understanding of letter and letter identification concepts and concepts of a syllable, a word, and a sentence.
- •Working with phoneme sounds by identifying and isolating phoneme sounds; categorizing phonemes; adding, deleting, and substituting; and blending and segmenting phonemes into their sound parts.

Hall and Moats (1998) have identified the stages of phonemic development in children. They report that by age three, most children should be able to recite simple rhymes, construct a rhyme from a given pattern, and identify alliterative sounds.

By the age of four, at least 50 percent of children can identify the syllables in a word, with the remaining 50 percent being able to do so by age five.

At six years of age, most children can match initial consonants, blend two or three phonemes, identify a rhyme, and determine the division between an onset and a rime in a word. Approximately 70 percent of these children can also count the phonemes in a word.

Yopp (1998) tells us that the two most critical skills for primary students to develop during the K-1 school years are the ability to segment words into their phonemic parts and blend word parts back into whole, recognizable words. By age seven, most children can blend three phonemes, segment three or four phonemes or blends, delete phonemes from words, and use phonetic spelling to write words they know. Children can generally segment words with consonant clusters by age eight and delete phonemes within clusters. Students who have fully developed these two skills are on the right path to becoming powerful readers.

Concepts of Print, Patterning, and Identifying Letter Names

The concepts of print are best learned by having the teacher model and discuss how books are handled and how print is read regularly. Using a pointer during read-aloud or "big book" time helps students see that print words and "talk" have a one-to-one correspondence. By tracking the pointer as the teacher reads, students can see that print is tracked across the page from top to bottom and from left to right.

Frequent modeling and time for children to practice imitating the teacher's handling books and reading to others help cement the concepts of print in each young learner. For disadvantaged children who have not grown up with books in the home, understanding the concepts of print and how books are read and handled is an essential skill.

Understanding the concepts of rhyme and alliteration is the subsequent skill children should be exposed to in the K-1 classroom. Children from enriched backgrounds with extensive reading in the home generally bring a strong understanding of language patterns and the concepts of rhyme and alliteration to the classroom.

Children from impoverished backgrounds or non-English-speaking cultures often need extensive exposure to language that contains rhyme, patterns, and alliteration. For non-English-speaking children, listening to the patterns and rhythms of English helps students learn the "lilt" or pattern of the English language.

Young children are specifically designed to filter out the sounds of the language they hear around them and quickly assimilate this language into their communication patterns. For students from disadvantaged homes or who are English language learners, extensive oral language and rich conversation must be modeled and heard daily.

Young children enjoy patterns and respond well to repetitious sounds in their environment. While all teachers should continue to read books with patterns, rhyme, and alliteration no matter what socioeconomic or cultural background their students come from, it is nonnegotiable for classrooms where students come from high-poverty or culturally diverse homes where English is not regularly spoken. Exposure to rich vocabulary in the classroom is necessary to help children expand their personal vocabularies and build background knowledge.

Pattern books help build phonemic awareness, extend vocabulary, and are enjoyable to primary children. By listening to books with patterns, such as the Martin and Carle *What Do You See* series of books, or an alliterative book like Martin's *Chicka, Chicka, Boom, Boom* (see resources for more suggestions of pattern and alliterative books appropriate for primary classrooms), students hear the richness of our language.

Choral or echo reading techniques work well with a pattern or predictable books. If the teacher uses questioning strategies to allow children to predict the pattern or provide a guess about a rhyming word, children increase their knowledge about rhyme and language rhythm.

Alliterative books heighten children's sensitivity to sounds and provide an engaging way to explore specific sounds in English. Some of these sounds are unique to English or are not found in a student's native language. For this reason, additional practice with these sounds helps facilitate pronunciation and vocal cord development.

Coaches can be helpful by providing teachers with suggestions of outstanding predictable and pattern books to fill out their classroom libraries. They can also help by collecting lists of these books and introducing teachers to new books they might enjoy sharing with their students.

The letters we use in English to read and write are simply symbols that we have come to accept for specific sounds in our language. Children must not only hear the specific sounds but also be able to identify the letters. To further complicate matters, not only do we use an uppercase alphabet, but we also use a lowercase alphabet which children must also learn to identify and be able to interchange in written form.

Adults often take this complex interconnectedness for granted because we are adept at recognizing both symbols for our alphabet. There is a funny story that illustrates this point quite humorously.

Many years ago, my school implemented an excellent, center-based, technology-assisted program from IBM called the "Writing to Read" program for K-1 students. Students rotated to one of five centers daily to learn foundational reading skills. In one center, students sat at computers and listened with headphones while specific letters were flashed on the screen. A pleasant woman's voice said, "This is the letter *A*. Say, '*A*.' Type the letter *A*." Students then repeated the name of the letter flashed before them on the screen and typed the indicated letter. Then the voice said, "The letter *A* says (short *A* sound), say (short *A* sound.). Type the letter *A*." Students then orally repeated the sound of the letter being displayed and again typed the letter.

As I was watching the children saying their letter names and typing the corresponding letters, one little boy had a perplexed look on his face and was intently staring at his computer keyboard. The little boy took off his headphones with a frown and motioned me to come over. "Yes?" I said expectantly. "Can I help you?"

The student said, "This lady is telling me to type that letter, and I don't see that letter!" With a scowl, he put his hands on his hips and stared at the keyboard.

I said, "Let me listen to see if I can help." I reached for the headphones and heard the voice say, "This is the letter *R*. Type *R*." As I looked at the screen, I realized that the computer was displaying the lower-case symbol "*r*" on the screen. The female voice kept requesting that the child type the corresponding letter name on the keyboard. Since the keyboard letter displayed all capital letters, the young man was right! Typing a lowercase r was an impossible task. No wonder he was frustrated.

The student returned to following the computer directions. After seeing the obvious problem, I said, "Well, you are right. That letter is not there," The boy smiled knowingly. I reached down to the keyboard and pushed the correct letter to continue the program. Fortunately, the next letter the program displayed was in capital form, so the boy continued his work.

I approached the aide in charge of the lab and said, "We have a problem." I explained what happened to the young man and his difficulty identifying a lowercase letter. We both laughed at the logic the boy had used. He was correct – he couldn't type the correct letter r he saw on the screen since it wasn't a match for any letter on the computer keyboard. The boy was right—the keyboard had no "r" symbol!

She nodded and said, "I have an idea. I can fix that." The next day when I stopped by the lab, our insightful aide had pieces of masking tape on each key showing the letter in both upper- and lower-case marker pen. It seems the wonderful programmers who designed this great program forgot that keyboards are designed only with upper-case letters. It reminded us how quickly we forget what learning all our letters from the beginning was like.

Children realize at an early age that adults use "letters" to write down what they want to say. Children want to learn to write their own names first, so they will often learn the basic shapes of the letters and their names. They may then combine these symbols with other "squiggles" and proudly report that they have "written" a letter or a note to someone they know.

Being able to recognize and identify the letters is a very different thing. Most children can say the names of the letters in their proper order or sing the alphabet song when they come to kindergarten since parents often practice this with their preschoolers. Most children can recognize and write approximately fourteen letters in kindergarten (Hiebert and Sawyer, 1984). This understanding must be fully developed in kindergarten since identifying the letter names is an essential developmental milestone for letter awareness and phonemic development.

Although children should learn to recognize and make both upper- and lowercase letters, begin by teaching the lowercase letters first. The lowercase letters are most commonly seen in picture books and primary reading materials. Children will see them in print more often than the uppercase letters. Once children have mastered the lowercase alphabet, then teach children to identify the uppercase alphabet as well.

When you teach the sounds of various letters, begin with at least one vowel so that students can begin making words as they learn letters. Once you have taught a vowel, begin with consonants with consistent sounds, such as b, j, k, m, n, p, s, and t, because they are easy to distinguish and hear. Do not simultaneously teach the sounds of similar letters, such as b and d; p and q; u and n; n and h; or m and n. Ensure children have completely mastered the first letter before introducing a similar letter that might be confused.

If students have difficulty hearing and differentiating sounds, you can construct simple "phonics phones" to help them amplify and clarify sounds. You can create inexpensive "sound phones" by gluing together one small straight PVC piece and 2 PVC elbows into the shape of an old-fashioned telephone handset. You can find these small PVP pipe pieces in the sprinkler section of your local home improvement store.

Phonics, sometimes called "whisper phones," help improve phonemic awareness and decoding. When students speak into them, the sound is amplified and funneled directly into the ear for improved hearing acuity. Phonics phones have also increased reading fluency and comprehension (Rasinski, 2002; Rasinski, Flexer & Boomgarden-Szypulski, 2006).

Children who have had frequent ear infections as preschoolers may have difficulty hearing sounds, so the additional amplification can be helpful to them as they learn the sounds associated with each phoneme. The additional clarity helps many children hear the sound you are trying to teach them more clearly. In my experience, it also helps children who may be more prone to attention deficit or learning disabilities focus more intently on the sounds they are saying and hearing.

Some children benefit from using manipulatives to improve their learning with difficulty differentiating between letters and sounds like b and d and p and q. In this case, raising a specific hand and saying the correct letter name or sound can help some children.

For example, children are asked to raise their left hand when saying the sound /b/ and their right hand when saying the sound /d/. Not only does this tactile signal help them better remember the sound, but it also helps them remember where to write the "stick" when writing a letter *b* or a letter *d*.

After reviewing this with children for a few days, I seldom have students who forget that the stick is written on the left for a letter *b* but on the right for a letter *d*. I also use the same "hand trick" when teaching the letters and sounds for *p* and *q*.

If children forget where the stick goes on a specific letter, a gentle reminder, "Which hand?" quickly reminds them to visualize the round shape of the letter with the stick on the correct side. Again, something to try for those having difficulty remembering which side the "stick" goes on for those particular letters.

While discussing hand movements and making concrete associations with abstract letters is a great strategy to teach all the letters.

Another effective strategy is to link tactile movements and objects (like animals or objects) to each letter. This helps children remember to connect the letter to the sound it makes. An example is A, apple, or Q, queen.

Several published programs provide this tactile-kinesthetic link, so you don't have to create connections yourself. I have seen many struggling readers make significant progress when a tactile element is added to learning, so I support any program that includes a tactile-kinesthetic element to help learn letters and sounds.

Children come to school with vast differences in experiential backgrounds. This is especially true in a kindergarten classroom. In addition to directly teaching the names of the letters, there should be places available where children can explore letters. Centers, where children can form or cut out letter shapes using play, dough, sand, salt, or shaving cream, are especially beneficial for those needing a more tactile experience.

In addition, having simple letter manipulatives such as magnetic letters, letter cards, or letter tiles available in a center for matching and forming words is also helpful. Teachers can also have students sort the letters by their features, such as upper-/lowercase; letters with curves/straight letters; consonants/vowels; letters with short sticks/letters with long sticks; and by colors if letters are colored. The more children play with and observe letters, the better their learning.

A quick assessment of a child's letter recognition skills is to display random letter cards to the child and ask them to identify the letters. The more children see, touch, and manipulate letter shapes, the more familiar and comfortable with them they will become. Children who recognize most upper- or lowercase letters are ready to move on to more advanced work with phonemes.

The Concepts of Syllable, Word, and Sentence

Once children can identify all of the letters and have assisted the teacher with making simple one-syllable words with a few carefully selected vowels and consonants, the teacher will want to begin introducing a few blends, such as "bl," "dr," and "st," and the common digraphs, such as "sh" and "th." As these letter combinations are introduced, the children continue to make words using these new letter combinations.

To help students understand the concept of a syllable, have children clap, tap, or use a musical instrument to identify the syllables as they repeat different words or names of children in the class. The teacher can also write words on cards and then use a pocket chart to sort words by the number of syllables it contains.

I am a believer in having children learn sight words. It is not because I think there is any magic in sight word reading itself, but, like learning math facts, when children can easily recognize some of the most common words they see in print, it helps reduce the cognitive load on their brains. It allows them to concentrate on the message of the text. When children have to spend extra time decoding common words, it slows them down and makes reading tiring and more complex.

Children can be introduced to a few "sight" words beginning in kindergarten. These include: a, I, it, the, and, in, of, to, he, she, is, on, that, and was. First-grade teachers should begin introducing children to the Dolch word list for 1st grade.

According to Moats (2000), the thirty most frequent sight words that 1st graders should know and be able to easily recognize are: the, you, said, his, to, they, were, do, know, was, would, are, some, your, of, there, because, as, mother, is, one, what, could, who, two, too, should, put, and whose. Every child should continue to practice these key essential sight words until they can recognize them quickly and without hesitation.

By the end of third grade, the key Dolch words should be mastered by every nondisabled primary child, even if they need intensive tutoring to make this possible. The more words children can recognize easily and quickly, the better fluency they will have when learning to read.

In addition to recognizing some specific sight words, children in K-1 should be asked to think about how many words are in various sentences. Children can count the words in short poems or the number of sentences in short passages. Teachers can also take time to count the words in the sentences composed by the class after they have written morning or afternoon messages or tapped out the syllables in specific sentences.

Children in second and third grades will progress to understanding the concept of the paragraph and how it is organized and constructed. The more children understand that text is simply "talk written down," the more prepared they will be to become fluent and thoughtful readers.

Phoneme Identification and Isolation

Generally, the first phonemic skill children acquire is the ability to hear specific phonemes in the beginning position of a word. Practicing this skill should be a primary target for kindergarten teachers. Since this skill is foundational, a quick assessment of a child's development in this area can indicate readiness for literacy instruction.

Teachers can help students develop this ability by asking questions like, "Who has a name that starts with the /b/ sound like in Bobby?" or they might ask, "Which sound is the same in the words 'bus,' 'bug,' and 'beautiful'?" Teachers can also ask children to listen for various initial sounds while listening to a story being read. For example, the teacher might say, "Listen for the /m/ sound as I read this story and raise your hand (or stand up) when you hear me say a word with the /m/ sound." Not only does this type of action raise children's sound awareness, but it has the added benefit of keeping the "wiggles" under control when young children have sat too long!

Another fun way of helping students practice identifying initial sounds is to sing to the tune of "Jimmie Crack Corn," "What is a word that starts with…?" followed by a verse that begins with "…is a word that starts with …." Children will love it and will ask to practice their song with new sounds as they learn them.

Another fun game that children will enjoy is a game called "Who Can See?" The teacher asks, "Who can see something in our room that starts with the sound /d/?" Children spot various items and respond with the name of the object. As children become proficient with identifying the initial sound, the teacher should then move to help them identify ending sounds followed by medial sounds.

Children must be able to hear, separate, and identify the individual phonemes to be successful with decoding. When students learn to identify a sound in a specific position, stay with one pattern to avoid confusion until children can easily identify sounds in that position. If students have trouble, use a mirror and/or the phoneme telephone described earlier to enhance the sounds that the child hears.

Purchase inexpensive letter tiles, or create them yourself by purchasing sheets of white wall tiles from the local home improvement center and adding letters with a permanent marker. Use the letters to help students create new words by changing initial sounds. For example, "cat" becomes "fat." "Fat" becomes "sat." "Sat" becomes "mat." "Mat" becomes "bat." "Bat" becomes "rat" and so forth. With this activity, children not only see that many words contain the same letter combinations, but they begin to realize just how vital recognizing the initial sound can be to understanding meaning. Elkonin boxes with letter tiles can also help children understand how sounds change as letters are exchanged.

When students have become adept at identifying the placement of various phonemes, the teacher can move to a more advanced skill where students categorize the phoneme sounds they hear. For example, the teacher might display the words "goat," "grass," "glass," and "sun," repeat them slowly, and then ask children to identify which word doesn't belong.

Using the reverse of this idea, the teacher might display the words "baby," "rug," "rabbit," "butterfly," "balloon," and "robot" and then ask students to assist in sorting them into the /b/ and /r/ sound categories. Pictures can also be helpful for these types of sorting activities. Again, since these activities are much more complex and higher level, they are best left until students have mastered identifying sounds in the beginning, ending, and medial positions of words.

Phoneme Blending and Segmenting

Once students can identify the position of phonemes, they are ready to move to blending and segmenting phonemes. By the end of kindergarten, this skill should be well-developed in most children. This skill is part of the foundation upon which effective reading is built, so no child should leave the first-grade classroom without this ability fully developed.

The inability to properly blend phonemes prevents children from being able to "sound out" and recognize words when first learning to read. This hampers them from becoming fluent and thoughtful readers as they advance into second and third grades.

Children must master this critical skill as early and as thoroughly as possible. As a coach, help first-grade teachers analyze their students to make sure that they are fully mastering this ability. Children who are struggling should receive intense assistance until they can blend and segment words easily and fluently.

Kindergarten teachers can begin teaching blending and segmenting orally using activities such as "Stretch and Snap." In this activity, the teacher stretches out a word by pronouncing it very slowly, phoneme by phoneme.

For example, the teacher might say, "Listen to this mystery word and try to see if you know what it is: /k/ /a/ /t/. Who can snap my word together and tell me what it is?" After children identify the word, the teacher may ask them to tap or clap out the sounds they hear in the word. Teachers can also interest children in identifying a mystery object placed in an opaque bag. The teacher can say, "I have some special items in my bag. I will put one in my hand and say its name very slowly. See if you can guess what the item I am holding is by listening carefully."

Another way to help students understand the concepts of blending and segmenting words into their phoneme parts is using four-part Elkonin boxes. The teacher selects words that contain only three or four phoneme sounds. As each sound is voiced, a marker representing that sound is moved into a box. The teacher draws one box per phoneme sound on an overhead transparency and places markers on the overhead equal to the phonemes in the selected word.

Students also have copies of an Elkonin mat at their desks and move markers representing the phonemes heard in the word as the teacher models this process for them. For example, for the word "fish," the teacher would draw three boxes and place three markers on the overhead stage. One chip would be slid into place for the /f/ sound, another for the /i/ sound, and a third to represent the /sh/ sound. The teacher would want to point out that even though the word "fish" has four letters, only three sounds are heard when the word is voiced.

Guide students with other words while students practice, either individually or with partners, saying the word and sliding the appropriate number of markers into the boxes. This tactile way of visualizing the sounds and thinking about the letters or letter combinations helps students understand that sometimes sounds are represented by only one letter. In contrast, letter combinations are required at other times to represent the sounds in the words we use.

Another visual strategy for helping children segment words is to place magnetic letters on the overhead projector. The teacher assists children with segmenting the word by placing pipe cleaners or pieces of string between the phonemes of each word. This same activity can also help children divide words into syllables or break apart compound words. This activity can continue well into the second and third-grade years as children learn more complex words and syllabification rules.

Another idea to help children visualize segmenting words into their phonemic sound parts is an activity known as "Chop the Word." The teacher and students hold their hands as if they were an ax. As the teacher says the word part by part, everyone "chops" the word at the appropriate stopping points. For example, the teacher might say /bu/ /ter/ /fly/ and make chopping motions after each phoneme segment. The teacher can then "snap" the word back together by clapping once and saying the entire word "butterfly." Children are asked to model the same action with the teacher and then on their own with different words.

As children become adept at blending and segmenting words, the teacher can also have children play a "Stump the Teacher" game. The children slowly sound out their words in this game and try to "fool" their teacher. The teacher, feigning confusion at times to increase the fun, "guesses" the mystery word students have presented in an elongated form. This strategy also helps teachers listen for misunderstandings and note children who continue to struggle with blending and segmenting words into their phonemic parts.

Phonics Instruction

The next essential component of effective reading is being able to decode words. Decoding is the ability to use visual, syntactic, and semantic clues to make meaning out of the words and sentences we read. A solid knowledge of phonic concepts helps readers quickly process the words they encounter while reading.

Visual clues are what we see when we look at the word. This consists of what letters make up the word and how they are arranged. The visual shape of a letter is what helps us distinguish if the word meaning should be interpreted as "dog," or "hog," or "bog."

Syntax is how the words are put together and the order in which we find them in a sentence. In a standard English sentence, prepositions follow a verb. For example, if someone said, "I to the store go," it would not make sense syntactically.

Semantic clues are how the word is used in the context of the sentence. Does it make sense with how it is being used? Does it make sense when considering the other elements of the sentence?

Each reading cueing system helps readers make meaning out of their words and sentences.

Reading expert Richard Allington (2001) says that "children should be engaged in *reading* more than they are engaged in *discussing* the act of reading." For this reason, phonics instruction should not take up more than 25 percent of the available reading time during the school day.

Phonics instruction should consist of an orderly, planned sequence that is systematically taught. A detailed discussion of teaching phonics is beyond the scope of this book. However, this discussion be found n my earlier book, *The Threads of Reading: Strategies for Literacy Development* (Tankersley, 2003).

By the end of first grade, children should have mastered the basic phonic constructions, such as initial and final consonant blends, vowel and consonant digraphs, long and short vowels, and *r*-controlled vowel patterns. As students progress in their understanding of how sounds fit together in English, their need for phonics instruction diminishes. In contrast, their need to practice those skills actively increases. Reading is a participation sport! Students get better at reading by reading. Practice improves performance.

Building Background Knowledge and Expanding Vocabularies

Providing high-quality preschool services is necessary for districts serving high-poverty homes if high-poverty students are ever expected to catch up to their more affluent peers. According to the research of Hart and Risley (2003), a gap between the vocabularies of affluent children and those of children from high-poverty homes develops as early as the age of three, with as much as a thirty-million to the thirty-two-million-word difference between the two groups of students. For this reason, primary teachers need to immerse children in word-rich environments when they enter school.

Without early exposure to words and rich language experiences, educators can expect children from high-poverty homes to start behind and stay behind their more advantaged peers throughout their school careers. Follow-up studies showed that even at the ages of five and nine, the high-poverty children continued to show the same oral language gaps that were evident at the age of three. This unfortunate imbalance will continue without intensive intervention early in a child's life. The larger a child's vocabulary, the more successful a reader they are likely to become.

Earlier in the chapter, we discussed ways teachers can create effective oral language environments that expand children's oral language skills. In addition to these strategies, primary teachers must also find ways to expand children's vocabularies explicitly and implicitly through extensive reading, wordplay, and rich classroom conversation.

Learning is about connecting what we already know about a topic to the new concepts or ideas being learned. Thus, to build vocabulary knowledge, we must help children connect what they already know to new words and concepts they are learning. It has been said that a picture is worth a thousand words, and this is absolutely true for children who come from high-poverty or non-English backgrounds. Often, these children lack background experiences that help them interpret new ideas and concepts unfamiliar to their world or lifestyle.

According to Marzano and Pickering (2005), "Many students acquire academic background knowledge outside of school and come to subject-area classes already knowing and using terms essential for understanding content...by contrast, students from families with fewer resources may have lacked such opportunities and, thus have not incidentally acquired important academic background knowledge" (p.3).

Pictures can help children make stronger connections to new concepts and ideas, especially for non-English-speaking students. For example, a child who lives in a desert community has little experience with forests or snow. Likewise, a child who lives in the northeastern part of the country might have no experience with tarantulas or desert lizards.

Word walls are a great way to help children deliberately learn and use new vocabulary. Word walls are areas of the classroom where the teacher features new words that children will find useful. Most teachers organize a word wall alphabetically and allow the word wall to grow over the course of the school year as new words are introduced. Adding words to our vocabulary requires many exposures to the new word over time, so seeing them posted on the classroom word wall helps to cement recognition.

Primary teachers should not only have a word wall but also take time to regularly work with the words by clapping out the letters, sounds, syllables, and spelling patterns. Associating syllables with a beat can help students to better learn the concept of syllables within words. Clapping games where children clap for each syllable the teacher says can help students understand how to divide words into syllables. Begin with two- or three-syllable words and build up to longer words with more syllables. This additional practice with the words and their syllable parts will help children learn them and reinforce the concepts of rime and phonic patterns commonly found in English words.

Children need to learn to quickly separate words into their onsets and rime patterns to be good decoders and spellers. When children think of the sounds associated with rime patterns that they know, they become better spellers. For example, by learning the rime "ump" students can change the onset and write the words "bump," "lump," "dump," and "stump," to name just a few. Nearly five hundred words can be derived from only thirty-seven rime patterns (Wylie and Durrell, 1970).

These rime patterns include ack, ain, ake, ale, all, ame, an, ank, ap, ash, at, ate, aw, ay, eat, ell, est, ice, ick, ide, ight, ill, in, ine, ing, ink, ip, ir, ock, oke, op, or, ore, uck, ug, ump, and unk.

Helping children recognize the basic patterns of these rimes helps them unlock many words in our language.

Working with children in late first, second, and third grades should include healthy activities, including forming words by manipulating onsets and rime patterns. When children can read the rime patterns quickly and easily, it increases fluency and, thus, comprehension.

While working with our students, some words must be explicitly taught. These words include vocabulary that is needed to understand a specific text. These specialized or scientific terms would not be known unless directly taught or specific words that students will see repeatedly. Many words have multiple
definitions in English, so we must ensure that children learn that the same word can have many meanings.

Primary students love using word webs, word maps, or similar graphic organizers to help them remember and understand new words. These tools can also help learners organize their thinking as they move into more content learning in the second and third grades. There are many wonderful resources for vocabulary graphic organizers on the Internet and in teacher supply stores. Literacy coaches can assist teachers to be more effective in this area by locating and sharing these resources with teachers.

Comprehension Building

When students first begin to learn to read, they concentrate mainly on decoding the words before them. This difficult and mentally challenging task detracts from the main purpose of reading: to make meaning from print (Clay, 1991). Because beginning readers use so much mental energy to attend to the print on the page, they have little fluency. They must concentrate on identifying the words first. As a result of this mental distraction, primary students must be reminded to "listen to the words" while reading. As students begin to decode and make meaning, primary teachers can help students with specific support during guided reading groups.

By the time children reach the third grade, there are already significant discrepancies between skills in an average classroom. Many students who struggle will never close the gap between themselves and their more advanced peers unless they receive targeted and appropriate intervention. Guided reading groups allow the teacher to provide the support necessary for students to read text slightly beyond their zone of proximal development (Vygotsky, 1978).

Students should be encouraged to read for fluency and comprehension first and foremost. To read fluently, students must decode rapidly and possess a large sight vocabulary of easily recognizable words. Successful readers easily and quickly recognize many words by sight, so they do not have to stop and decode every word while reading a text.

Children should also commit the common sight words to memory to devote their cognitive energy to making sense of the text they read. Dolch or Fry sight word lists can help children develop strong automaticity with core common vocabulary words. Good readers also anticipate "filler" words in contexts while reading.

If children make minor substitutions during reading, like reading the word "the" for "a" or similar misreading that do not change the essential meaning of the passage, they should not be stopped or corrected. This is using good anticipation skills while reading. If a student misreads a word that does alter the meaning of the sentence, then the teacher should call the student's attention to the problem and ask them to "try that sentence again." during reading.

Asking children to stop and reread words that do not impact meaning can cause children to slow down their reading. It can contribute to "word by word" reading as the child makes sure they decode each word perfectly. Good reading is not about reading every word perfectly; it is about understanding the sentence's meaning.

Using Technology to Strengthen Primary Literacy

Most of the children coming to school in this era are tech-savvy. They are comfortable with cell phones, iPods, iPads, and laptop computers. Now hundreds of books and useful apps are available for small devices such as the iPad to help students read online, master letters and sounds, and build their reading skills. Students can now read interactive books online at the website https://www.starfall.com or write stories online with sites such as https://www.meddybemps.com or https://storylineonline.net name just a few. Incorporating technology into the classroom to keep the children of the twenty-first century engaged and productive is an excellent way to increase students' access to books.

Effective reading coaches should research the best sites and pass these suggestions to teachers to use with their students and share information around the school. Work closely with your district technology director or coordinator to help teachers identify and get access to appropriate literacy sites that can strengthen classroom instruction.

Besides using technology to promote reading and writing, teachers can use the excellent Web sites of many children's book authors as special draws for student interest. Many authors, like Roald Dahl, Tomie dePaola, and Mercer Mayer, to name just a few, have excellent Web sites with great activities for young children.

Teachers can set up centers where their students learn about an author, their works, and a bit about their life. I recently watched two 2nd-grade children working in a wonderful center built around author Robert Munsch. The two boys were working independently as partners, following directions on a task card the teacher placed in the center. The students first read several of the Munsch books on display. They then logged on to the computer in the center and read several Robert Munsch poems from the author's Web site. They then selected one of the poems to illustrate with their own drawing. Once they had completed their readings and the drawing, they located the author's address in the contact link. They wrote a draft letter to Robert about his work.

Throughout the entire time, the children were engaged and excited about Robert's work and the authentic and meaningful work they had been asked to do. This is a great way to introduce children to the fact that real people write books and that their favorite authors have often written many books they might enjoy.

Independent Reading in the
Primary Grades

Classrooms should always have many reading materials, such as books, charts, posters, labels, magazines, writing and stamping centers, and other print materials for primary students to see and explore. There should be decodable books and authentic text available for student use.

Classrooms should have an abundant supply of both fictional and nonfictional selections available for student enjoyment. Students should be given time daily, especially in second and third grades, to read these materials and interact with one another about what they have read to develop the habit of handling print on a regular basis.

As a reading coach, you can help teachers examine their daily schedules to see where some additional free reading time can be provided on a daily basis so that children can spend more time actually doing reading rather than talking about reading. Remember, reading is a "participation sport" that only improves with practice. The more students read, the more proficient they will become at "doing" reading.

Suggest to teachers that the "big books" they have used during shared reading time be available to students during an independent reading time if possible. Whenever big books are read and shared by the teacher, these books become special favorites of students, and children want to read them repeatedly. These books are often referred to as "blessed books" since the teacher has given tacit approval or "a blessing" by using them as whole-class read-aloud books. Children naturally want to read and explore these books over and over whenever possible.

Encourage teachers to consider placing these books on an easel accompanied by a small pointer so that students can model taking the role of the teacher and "reading" these books to their peers. At the start of the year, be sure that the teacher models how to appropriately handle and read the book in the big book reading area so that students are clear on how they will behave.

Developing Writing Skills

Students learn about writing by watching adults write. For this reason, teachers should model writing daily for students. Many K-1 teachers begin their day with a "Morning Message," where students and their teacher compose a joint message in narrative or letter format about planned daily events or activities on the whiteboard or on a sheet of chart paper. For example, students and teachers may jointly compose the following morning message about the day's intended activities as a morning message on chart paper. Not only does the morning message model good writing skills, but it can also be reviewed periodically as a type of class journal.

Dear Class,

We will have a lot of fun learning new information today. Today, we will study butterflies in science class. We will sing our favorite songs when we go to music class. We will draw a picture of our favorite book character from Charlotte's Web. Yesterday, we went to PE and played soccer. We also looked at a big globe to see where we live in social studies.

Yours Truly,

Mrs. Smith

Many teachers use collaborative writing to model proper writing techniques and help students think about the days of the week, weather conditions, special guests or projects, and upcoming events. This activity can also help students understand how to record information for their journal writing.

Teachers can also use "modeled writing" or "pattern writing" activities to help students explore the idea that reading is "talk written down." For example, the teacher might have students complete a simple sentence stem such as "I like…" or "I am grateful for…" as she records each student's response to the starter stem on a chart. The same collaborative message-writing technique can also be used to write a daily "Closing Message," where the teacher guides students in writing about the key events and activities of the instructional day.

Class books are popular with students and are inexpensive to make available to students for their reading practice. Some teachers extend this into a book-writing activity by writing each sentence on a book page and having the child illustrate their own page with their contribution. The completed pages are then bound into a classroom book with a honeycomb binder and placed in the student reading center for all students to enjoy and read during independent reading time.

Journaling should be a daily activity in all K-3 classrooms. Daily journaling can significantly enhance a student's writing ability and understanding of symbolic language. From kindergarten, students should be given their own writing journal and encouraged to "write" for a specific amount of time. For preliterate students, this may consist of drawing pictures with a few random letters strategically placed on the page.

For children in second and third grades, writing about stories and other academic content should definitely become a part of the daily activities of each classroom. For more advanced students, particularly as they become more familiar with story form and hear engaging stories, story writing may emerge by the early months of first grade.

Help teachers examine student writing development regularly since student progress can often show teachers' understanding that children are developing. These simple assessments can then help teachers determine future instructional needs and goals.

Every K-1 classroom should be equipped with a "writing center" where there are plentiful writing supplies, such as pencils, markers, paper of various types, stamps and stamp pads, write-on boards with erasers, and even age-appropriate computer keyboards or electronic word devices for students to use and explore. The writing center might also contain sets of alphabet tiles or other tactile writing surfaces, such as sandboxes, for students to practice writing and sharing words.

Tactile writing stimulus can significantly benefit children with strong tactile learning needs, such as special-needs students. Students can also be exposed to online writing Websites such as https://lulujr.com.; https://www.storyjumper.com; or https://storybird.com (and others), where students can write and illustrate their personal books. They can then proudly read their books to friends and family alike.

Assessing and Analysing Reading Progress

To determine kindergartners' print readiness, an excellent assessment is Marie Clay's Concepts of Print tests (Clay, 2006). These short tests identify whether young children understand directionality knowledge (top to bottom, left to right, and front to back. They also assess a student's knowledge of handling a book and similar foundational print concepts. Students from impoverished backgrounds may lack these skills when they come to school, so teachers should plan lessons that introduce and develop these essential understandings early in the school year.

Three types of assessments can be used to assess reading progress. The first type of reading test is a screening assessment. The second is diagnostic assessments, and the third is progress monitoring assessment tools.

One of the best ways to determine what primary students know and can do is to administer an "oral reading record" or "running record" to beginning and developing readers (Clay, 1972). If you have not been trained to administer and interpret a running record, it is a skill you should acquire. By noting the mistakes, substitutions, or hesitations a student makes while reading, teachers can identify what phonic concepts a child understands and which ones they lack. Then, they can determine the most logical instructional steps to take with that child. Children with like needs can be grouped and provided with appropriate instruction to help them further develop their reading skills. Teachers in primary grades should also be trained to administer and interpret the data from a child's running record.

While running records are helpful ways to monitor student progress, teachers do not always understand how to use running record data to plan their instruction. Many classroom teachers who have not been trained extensively in reading do not fully understand how to interpret the information obtained from analyzing a child's reading record.

Some teachers do not know how to analyze the information they can get from these assessments. They don't know how to use the summative data to guide and shape their classroom instruction. This is a place where the literacy coach can help by showing reluctant teachers how to properly administer a running record, analyze the performance of various students, and then use this information to plan directed lessons to serve the students' needs.

Literacy coaches should take time to learn as much as possible about analyzing student performance and assessing reading behaviors. There are many good books on interpreting and correcting reading miscues and difficulties. I particularly like *Miscue Analysis Made Easy: Building on Student Strengths* by Sandra Wilde (2000), *Reading Miscue Inventory: From Evaluation to Instruction* by Yvetta Goodman (2005), and *Locating and Correcting Reading Difficulties* by Shanker and Ekwall (2008). Each volume would be helpful additions to your professional coaching library. These books could help you better assist classroom teachers when interpreting running records and using the data to help teachers plan appropriate instruction.

Primary Reading Development

The kindergarten year should be when a solid foundation for reading is firmly built. Primary students should understand how to handle a book and track print on a page. They should be able to isolate at least a word's beginning and ending sounds and change the beginning sound to make a new word. By the end of kindergarten, children should know all the letter names and be able to name at least one sound for each letter.

Finally, kindergartners must be able to orally blend and segment the sounds they hear in ways that have been discussed in this chapter. Without these foundational skills, the child will only drop further and further behind as first-grade teachers begin to help children apply these skills to their beginning reading.

If a child cannot do any of these things by the time they approach the middle of the kindergarten school year, then intensive tutoring should occur with that child. Unless there is a specific learning disability requiring alternative instruction, no child should ever leave kindergarten without mastering these essential skills.

First grade is a time of tremendous reading growth. This is the year children link the letters on the page to words and sentences. During this time, the child transitions between making up words that fit the pictures on the page and decoding the words on the page. This should be when children learn to apply their oral understandings and new blending and segmenting skills to print on the page.

By the end of first grade, the child should be able to identify familiar sounds and common text patterns and sound out unknown words in grade-level text. They should also be beginning to build a sight word vocabulary with simple words such as "have," "said," " there," "why," and similar words. The child should be able to represent the most commonly understood words with phonemic approximations that are pretty close to the actual spelling and have at their command a good list of words that can be spelled correctly.

The child should be able to express thoughts in writing and understand the concepts that sentences begin with capital letters, that words need spaces between them and that sentences end with punctuation, which tells the reader about the sentence. The child should be able to predict what will happen next in a story, briefly summarize the text, and provide justifications for their thoughts and ideas about the text.

The child should be able to connect their background understandings to the text being read, answer simple comprehension questions, and retell the significant events of a story they have read or heard.

The first-grade year is a great time to get parents involved to encourage and support good reading behaviors so that their children become lifelong, strong, and capable readers. By the end of the first-grade year, the child on track with reading development has made substantial strides toward becoming a fluent and capable reader.

Children learn to develop fluency and apply their newly learned decoding skills in the second and third grades. In second grade, children begin using textbooks as reading sources and learning to process all types of print regularly.

By the end of second grade, children can read more sophisticated texts and are developing an understanding of multisyllabic words in their reading. At this stage, children begin to read both nonfiction and fiction. They learn to read information from diagrams, charts, and graphs and can recall facts and details they have read in the text.

During second grade, children can see similarities and differences. They can also connect and compare information from several texts. They correctly spell most sight words and can accurately read many irregularly spelled words in context. They have mastered most decoding skills and understand how to break a word into word parts or syllables to try to identify meaning. They understand that writing aims to communicate meaning, and they can begin to organize information into simple forms, such as a report, a letter, or a journal entry.

Children in this developmental stage ask questions and can give possible responses to how, why, and what-if questions based on a text that they have read. By the end of 2nd grade, many children are ready to move into simple "chapter books" and readily self-select reading material that interests them. While they still may enjoy being read to occasionally, more and more children at this stage are taking on their own reading and book selection. This is an excellent time to help children explore their interests and continue practicing reading authentic texts.

By third grade, children should be reading reasonably fluently and have a good command of the reading process. They should be independently reading longer fiction books containing chapters and be able to learn by reading. Children should be able to summarize the major points from fiction or nonfiction and identify a story's central theme or message.

Children in third grade should be able to ask "how," "why," and "what-if" types of questions about nonfictional text and use the information to express opinions or make hypotheses. In writing, the child should be able to write and combine information from multiple sources into a report format.

The second and third-grade years should be all about learning to become a quick and able decoder who reads with fluency and comprehension. Third-grade students should be able to review their own writing for spelling and grammar and make revisions to improve their writing. The end of 3rd grade marks the end of "learning to read."

From fourth grade on, children are expected to read more independently and to use "reading to learn." as the literacy coach,

you can help teachers understand the developmental stages of readers in grades K-3. You can use the ideas in this chapter to help teachers instruct their children more effectively
and help them spot difficulties quickly before children fall too far behind in their reading development.

Conclusion

In this chapter, we have discussed the elements that should be found in dynamic and effective reading classrooms at the K-3 level. These ideas should be a starting place to assist classroom teachers in reflecting upon their current literacy practices. While we have only scratched the surface of these ideas in this brief chapter, this material can help literacy coaches open dialogue with classroom teachers about areas for potential personal growth and collaborative work between teacher and coach.

In the resources section, you will find a self-assessment that you can share with primary teachers to help them evaluate their classroom environment and the various instructional strategies they may be using. These instruments can help primary teachers target areas to emphasize or improve upon during their coaching time.

To get teachers' feedback, provide a copy of the survey, ask teachers to reflect on each question, and privately rank themselves. Unless you have a trusting relationship with the teacher, please do not ask to see their personal rankings. Ask each teacher to provide you with two or three prioritized goals based on their self-reflection. Once they have completed the self-reflection, ask them to think about areas where they would like assistance, more information, or targeted coaching. Once they have identified their areas of interest, develop specific and measurable goals that you and your colleague agree upon and can use to guide your work.

"If we want to help teachers understand why they do what they do, we must anchor their thinking in the same cognitive processes they want to instill in their students."
Lyons and Pinnell (2001, p. 118)

Chapter 2
Literacy Development for Teachers in Grades 4-8

The Productive Literacy Environment for Students in Grades 4-8

Reading instruction in the primary grades is mostly about learning to read, develop vocabulary, and decode. In contrast, instruction in grades 4-8 focuses more on developing fluency, expanding vocabulary knowledge, and establishing strong comprehension skills. During these crucial years, students learn to link the words on the page to the language they already know to understand what they have read.

Many reading teachers say that instead of "learning to read" during the middle grades, students are now "reading to learn" and expanding their content knowledge. From fourth grade, students will be expected to use their reading skills to learn and process information thoughtfully and analytically. During these critical middle-level years, students must become fluent readers who can devote their cognitive energy to understanding and making meaning out of the text. Let's peek into three outstanding teachers' classrooms to learn more about productive literacy environments at the 4th- through 8th-grade level.

What Does Effective Reading Instruction Look Like in Grades 4-8?

♋

Visiting Sondra - Grade 4

The first classroom we will visit is Sondra's fourth-grade class. Sondra has been teaching for over ten years and has a master's degree in reading from her local university. She serves as a grade-level chair and loves to coordinate special activities such as school plays and reading events for the school.

Sondra's room is always bustling with noise and high engagement, but it is clearly organized and on-task. Sondra's room is alive with colored pictures of characters from various books, vocabulary words, and student work on the walls. She has shelves and shelves of nicely organized tubs of books with genre labels clearly displayed on the front of each tub.

The desks in her room are organized into tight sets of four with a large free space area on one side of the room. A chair with a large, comfortable rug is tucked away in the back corner. A small, well-organized teacher's desk is tucked back against the wall in the other corner, with a teacher chair and a student chair that she uses for regular literature and writing conferences with students. We also see a bulletin board with interesting words, word puzzles, and a content word wall that looks as if it regularly receives new words as students progress through their content textbooks.

We see several groups of students huddled in different parts of the room, practicing a readers' theater presentation again and again to perfect their delivery. Sondra flits from group to group, listening in and providing encouragement and suggestions. The children are clearly enjoying themselves and are very attentive to their work.

The children also give each other feedback and model how to read various passages as they work. Sondra's gentle smiles, frequent thumbs-up encouragement, and pats on the back clearly make the children smile and work even harder to perfect their delivery of the text. Sondra reminds the class that their characters must sound "like real talking," so they should think about how real people would say the material in their scripts—not just read it in a flat or "boring" voice.

As most groups complete several practice runs through their assigned text and appear to read their passage reasonably fluently, Sondra signals that they are to return to their seats. She then pulls four high stools to the open area of the classroom. She takes a container and asks one child to draw the name of the first group that will present their readers' theater presentation to the class.

As the first group of four settles in front of the class on the stools, another student sets up a video camera tripod and takes his place as the class videographer. Sondra reminds the audience that their role is to keep notes on what the readers are doing well. She whispers that she uses the videotapes to observe each reader more closely and note their progress as they read their part of the text. She also posts some of the videos on her classroom Web site for parents to enjoy. She smiles and says that this helps parents see how their child reads compared to others but helps them feel more involved with classroom activities.

As the first group finishes their presentation with a bit of nervous laughter, Sondra asks students to give the readers compliments on their rendition. Students begin their compliments with "I like the way you…" and offer several comments to the group.

After each group has given their text renditions, Sondra asks her students to briefly discuss with their group what they could do to improve their own readings and make them more engaging. As we tiptoe out of the room, Sondra tells the students that tomorrow, they will be reading a story and creating their own readers' theater script with their working group.

Visiting Juan – Fifth Grade

Next, we will visit Juan's fifth-grade class. We see many student-drawn graphic organizers posted on the classroom walls as we enter the room. The organizers contain literary information and notes from all content areas that students have been studying.

We see fifth-grade vocabulary terms on another wall with student-drawn pictures next to each term. It is clear from looking at the words and pictures that the pictures help students recall the meaning of the term. Each word also has a definition for the word written in the student's own words. Students have created a meaningful definition that connects to the context where the word was found.

A few words with multiple meanings are attractively displayed in a bubble map graphic organizer. A long list of vocabulary clearly related to the Civil War is clustered on one side of this vocabulary wall. On another wall, we see a collection of affixes and root words, their meanings and origins, and a poster that lists "fix-up" strategies for students to use when meaning is lost. It is clear that Juan spends a lot of time helping his students think about words, understand words at different levels, and understand the etymology behind the words they use in their learning.

Juan's desk, located at the back of the room, contains a series of labeled, stacked trays where students submit various types of work during the day. We can see that Juan does not spend much time in this area since tubs of leveled books are stacked up on the top of the desk. Student desks are organized into four groups to allow for easy group access. Students appear comfortable with this arrangement and work well with their group partners.

Juan has attached a long, butcher-paper timeline of key Civil War events on another classroom wall. The handwriting shows that students have added key details and created illustrations of these events while learning about the Civil War. We see several more well-organized tubs of books on the back counter of the classroom.

The tubs are labeled with various topics, such as fantasy, space, famous people, science, humor, animal stories, and so forth, and contain books of all types and genres. In another tub are magazines and, in yet another tub, a large selection of well-worn comic books of all types.

A large foam mat sits in one corner of the room, serving as a small student reading area. On the mat are a few large, red pillows that students use to support their backs while leaning against the wall in this comfortable reading center. A mobile with famous people from the Civil War era, such as Ulysses S. Grant and Robert E. Lee, dangles above the reading center. A small tub of books related to this historical period sits on a low stand next to the reading area. Several of the books have bookmarks sticking out of them.

As we enter the room, students read and discuss several diary articles. The articles have been written from the perspective of various Union and Confederate people (solider, politicians, slaves, and business/property owners). Juan explains that each group has a packet of articles written from various viewpoints that he has asked students to read.

Juan whispers that he allows the students in each group to decide if they will read the articles aloud to one another in soft voices or read them silently. He points to a group who have just moved to the reading center and now have their heads together, quietly reading aloud to one another.

Another group sits on the carpet in another corner of the room, discussing how they want to read the articles. Other groups are reading the articles silently at their desks. Juan points to the whiteboard and tells us that each group has been asked to answer the three posted questions.

The questions are: 1) How was life different for people living in the North and South? With your group, create a graphic organizer on your chart paper to display and organize your findings; 2) After reading and thinking about what each person's diary article says, discuss each person's viewpoint with your group. With your group, choose one viewpoint that best explains life during this time. Then reflect on each viewpoint that you read. Identify three adjectives to describe how each person views the war; and 3) Which side would you be on if you had lived in this time? What would you do if you found yourself against other family members, such as a brother or uncle from your family? Could you fight against your brother or uncle in battle? What makes you think so? As a group, create a convincing argument you might give another family member about your position on this difficult decision.

As groups begin to finish their packet of readings, a lively discussion ensues in each group. We notice that there are English language learners spread around the various groups. They are engaged and actively participate in the discussions at their tables. Juan smiles and says that since incorporating these types of high-level reading, writing, and thinking strategies in all content areas, more ELL children now demonstrate English proficiency on the state language assessment than in any other fifth-grade classroom in his school.

As we observe, we notice that no one seems shy about contributing to the discussion in any group. We can clearly see that Juan's students are engaged and eagerly involved in their learning in this classroom. Juan waves and smiles as we quietly slip out the door and move down the hall to the seventh-grade wing.

Visiting Michelle – Seventh Grade ELA

We travel next to Michelle's 7th-grade language arts class. As we enter, we see that Michelle's students are seated in groups of four around six round tables. Her classroom is bright and cheery. Colorful book jackets and pictures of authors are posted around the walls.

We see a large quantity of student writing posted on one of the walls. As we look closer at the writing, we see that students have written an essay to describe which of Poe's stories they find the most interesting and why. A bulletin board with a large picture of Edgar Allan Poe is on another wall, surrounded by some student-created dust covers of Poe's books. There are also several acrostic poems using some of the words in Poe's short stories posted there.

The students have iPads and are engrossed in their reading. Michelle says the students are reading a chapter from *The City of Ember* by Jeanne DuPrau. She tells us that the library has ample online books that students can use on the classroom set of iPads. Students have just finished a unit on Edgar Allan Poe and are now starting a unit on fantasy works with this new novel.

She says the class can now access most of the newer works on their iPads, so she can use more literature than ever with her students. She is trying to focus on more contemporary literature that hooks student attention and meets the required readings of her district. Poe is one of the district-mandated authors she is required to study. Michelle says that with the iPads, she can easily blend district requirements and more contemporary literature into her curriculum. She says her student scores have never been higher since using this blended approach. Her principal is happy with her teaching style and how students are improving their reading skills.

As we look over a student's shoulder, we see him use an electronic "sticky note" to write a question and place it on the electronic page he is reading. Michelle smiles and tells us each student has specific tasks to complete as they read the text.

She asks students to use the electronic sticky notes to mark interesting words or phrases and note their questions as they read. Students will also attach an electronic note when they identify passages that remind them of something they have experienced or read about in another text or when they connect with something happening in the world.

In the center of each table is a list of predictions that each group created before reading. The list outlines what they think might happen on the selected pages. At the bottom of the list, students have also written a couple of questions about what the characters might do or what might happen in the section. It is clear from the form that students will verify the accuracy of their predictions by placing check marks in a "true" box on the form.

When students finish their reading, Michelle tells us that her students will get into their groups to share their interesting words and phrases and the insights and connections they made while reading. After discussing the contents of their electronic notes, each team will share key group insights or observations with the class.

Key vocabulary may also be identified and added to the classroom word wall as groups identify keywords they have found in the text that they think are important. They might also ask questions they still have about the material they have read that were not answered during their group discussions. We thank Michelle for a wonderful visit and leave her busy classroom.

Traits of Effective Readers in Grades 4-8

As we have seen from the descriptions of these three classrooms, middle school readers also need positive, supportive, and risk-free environments where they are free to explore, question, and learn about the world of print. In effective literacy classrooms, a strong presence of books and print is clearly apparent from the moment one enters the classroom.

Technology such as interactive whiteboards, digital cameras, document cameras, laptops, online books, and iPads is readily available and integrated into ongoing instruction, allowing many avenues of research and expression.

We can easily see that the classroom contains various print resources, such as magazines, newspapers, short stories, pamphlets, brochures, books on tape/CD, comic books, online resources, cartoons, and manuals of all types to suit various interests. Some classrooms may have comfy reading areas with beanbags, couches, or overstuffed chairs that encourage students to curl up with books during free reading time.

Others may use flexible gathering areas or table settings where students can come together to work or discuss what they are learning in various content areas. No matter what the classroom's configuration, it is clear that reading is a popular and valued activity in the classroom.

A substantial amount of time is spent reading, doing research by reading, or talking about what has been read. The teacher guides and shapes the highly focused work and provides feedback in each classroom. It is clearly the students who are engaged in the reading and learning.

We have seen from peeking into these three classrooms that teachers in grades 4-8 help students develop a sense of print using a combination of processes. Younger fourth-grade readers like those we learned about in Sondra's class need to build strong fluency skills and expand their vocabularies so that as they grow and develop, they can also focus on building strong comprehension skills. They must be reminded to use their decoding and "fix-up" skills as they encounter more complex literary texts and content reading materials.

Sondra created a supportive and encouraging atmosphere where there was not only teacher evaluation but also peer and self-evaluation taking place. Word walls and vocabulary development helped students expand their vocabulary and connect meaning to text. Rehearsal is a key strategy to refine performance and improve student fluency. She used video to analyze student performance. It also provided a connection for parents so they could also analyze their child's level of performance.

For fourth and fifth-grade students, becoming fluent readers who understand how to approach, process, and comprehend text is non-negotiable. The time for learning to decode text must now give way to refining their comprehension skills and higher-order thinking skills. Students must learn to visualize their reading and follow the sequence or storyline during this time. They must also monitor their own level of understanding as they read and have an array of "fix-up" strategies to use when meaning has been lost. Active engagement in meaning must be the goal of comprehension instruction.

As we observed in Juan's 5th-grade classroom, effective middle-grade classrooms buzz with student discussions, collaborative projects, and students sharing ideas and thoughts. Students are frequently engaged in reading as individuals to facilitate the development of effective comprehension and higher-order thinking skills. They also read within small groups and participate in reading as a class. Reading instruction goes on during the official language arts period. It is integrated into all content areas during the day to strengthen and build strong and effective readers.

Students can be seen assisting one another with new vocabulary, making and verifying predictions, asking questions, making notes, and interpreting what they have read to each other and their teacher. The teacher and their students often stop to think aloud on various topics throughout the school day as they work to ensure good comprehension.

Students were fully immersed in "reading to learn" by exploring the Civil War-era diary entries. Graphic organizers, illustrations, student definitions, and the study of word parts and word etymology helped students expand their understanding of words, their usage, and their origins.

The use of groups where struggling readers and ELL learners were encouraged to engage in meaningful and authentic conversation around text helped increase the understanding of all students.

The teacher encouraged students to use higher-order thinking about the content by comparing and contrasting, examining viewpoints, or making personal connections. This helped strengthen student skills and enhanced student interest in the lesson content.

Skilled readers have schemata for topics and draw on them as they read. They have experience with text structure, metacognitive processes, vocabulary, word etymology, and the syntax of language. Skilled readers link prior knowledge with the new knowledge they are learning. Their teachers understand that reading is the interaction of all these processes. They design lessons to help students learn, refine, and apply these skills.

In Michelle's classroom, we again saw a collaborative and safe atmosphere where students were exposed to more "traditional" content and more contemporary, "high-interest" materials. Students applied their comprehension skills by predicting, questioning, and connecting to text in many personal ways.

The use of technology expanded the teacher's options and provided a motivating way to read and respond to text. She met her district's curriculum expectations and stimulated student interest by using newer online resources that provided high engagement and further reinforced the standards she was expected to teach her students.

Providing Support for Teachers in 4 - 8

First, let's reflect on the classroom learning environment. Effective classrooms that build strong literacy skills in students in grades four through eight generally exhibit a warm, open, and inviting classroom climate. This is a classroom where children can take risks and receive support from a helpful and caring adult who demonstrates a love of learning. Middle-grade children learn best in a positive, stress-free environment encourages risk-taking, curiosity, and exploration.

Consider the following characteristics as you think about the 4th through 8th-grade classroom environment. The reading coach can use a list of questions to help teachers in grades four through eight reflect and select areas to target for growth and development.

- Does the classroom have a warm, positive, and supportive atmosphere in the room at all times?
- Does the room have a variety of types and levels of books (i.e., fiction and nonfiction, high interest-low vocabulary, reference, audiobooks, magazines, comic books, online books) available to students?
- Is there an area where students can share book recommendations and reviews of reading materials?
- Is there a shared reading area for reading aloud or an individual reading area that students may use to relax and enjoy a book during independent reading time?
- Are there print materials and images representative of the cultures and races of classroom populations visible in the room?
- Is there abundant high-quality, literacy-related student work posted on the classroom walls and bulletin boards?
- Do students and teachers enjoy one another's company, and do students appear willing to take risks? Do students display relaxed self-confidence when approaching tasks?

Next, we will consider the components of a literacy-rich classroom, which include general literacy elements, vocabulary development, fluency development, the development of comprehension and higher-order thinking skills, and, finally, strengthening writing skills and establishing the links between writing and reading. The following list of characteristics should be evident in the fourth through eighth-grade classroom. Here are questions to analyze the overall literacy instruction taking place in the classroom:

- Does the teacher help students reflect on their reading habits and interests? Does the teacher provide opportunities for students to explore and grow as independent and capable readers?
- Does the teacher include a wide variety of text levels in the classroom?
- Does the teacher use traditional and text-based readings and timely articles or contemporary fiction when appropriate for instruction?
- Does the teacher thoughtfully organize lessons to include reading goals and strategies before, during, and after?
- Does the teacher help students set purposeful goals for content reading?
- Does the teacher flexibly group and regroup students according to instructional needs?
- Does the teacher use appropriate assessments and regular observations to guide student needs, guided reading work, and flexible grouping practices?
- Does the teacher provide support to build student self-confidence and increase reading persistence?

•Do struggling readers have additional support within the class-room to help them close the gap between their current performance level and grade-level expectations? Does the school have Tier 2 and Tier 3 RTI support for those who need more intensive help? Does the teacher use these supports to ensure early literacy success?

•Does the teacher use appropriate technology to promote student interest and excitement in reading?

In addition to these broad questions, you will want to help the teacher analyze fluency and vocabulary development instruction, comprehension and higher-order reading, and connecting writing to reading.

The charts in the resources section can help you and the teacher analyze teacher performance in each area. These areas can also serve as the basis for collaborative goal-setting. Provide the survey to each teacher you work with and encourage them to complete the self-evaluation privately. Ask them to write down two or three areas where they want coaching assistance in the next few months. Together, you will write these into S.M.A.R.T. goals to be mutually worked on during the year.

Creating written goals will help you focus everyone's attention on what needs to be improved. It will also help you better track each teacher's professional development plans. Make sure that your goals are observable and measurable to track progress.

Building Student Literacy in Grades 4 - 8

Teacher Read-Alouds

People of all ages love to be read to, so teachers should read aloud for at least ten to thirty minutes daily. When students hear text read aloud, they can access text at a higher level than they might be able to on their own. This can help stimulate interest in reading a particular topic or genre, build vocabulary, and enhance background knowledge.

Reading aloud is especially helpful for English language learners or students from high-poverty backgrounds. These students need to hear spoken language regularly to further develop their listening abilities and build vocabulary.

Students can also learn to use more appropriate pacing, expression, and tone and add interest to their reading by listening to their teacher model these essential qualities. Before reading, always activate the student's prior knowledge of the subject and help them connect to the new material as you read orally.

Building Fluency

Reading is a "participation sport." This means that, like any other sport, one must practice reading to become stronger. We often see that too much time is spent "practicing" the components of reading at the expense of encouraging students to spend time reading. I can't be more precise when I say that the more a child reads, the better reader they become.

Conversely, the less a child reads, the more difficult reading becomes for the child. Students who don't read are more likely to struggle as the material becomes more difficult. If reading is not done regularly, we begin to lose some of our skill and efficiency.

This increases the gap between good readers and poor readers as students move through the grades.

Children must practice reading regularly and continuously so that decoding becomes automatic. Students who struggle with reading are likelier to avoid reading as much as possible. This vicious cycle is what continues to keep children from becoming fluent and effective readers.

While we may think that we are great multitaskers, the reality is that the brain has difficulty focusing on decoding and comprehension simultaneously. To be efficient and effective at reading, a reader cannot simultaneously focus on decoding and processing meaning. If a reader's attention is focused on understanding the words, then there is little cognitive energy left to understand the text's message.

Fluency improves as readers become more automatic in decoding words and linking information to their background knowledge. When students do not have to pay as much attention to decoding words they are reading, more cognitive energy can be devoted to making meaning from the text. Students can focus on the author's overall meaning when they can process text easily and accurately.

A large body of research has shown that students improve reading fluency by practicing extensively with texts at their independent reading level. This is where they can read a text without teacher assistance in a text where they have at least 95 percent accuracy in word recognition.

One of the most beneficial ways to increase fluency is to practice reading the same passage at an appropriate level of difficulty several times, referred to as "rereading." the more we "rehearse" or reread a specific passage, the better we understand it. Rereading allows a reader to maximize understanding, focus on expression, and minimize the work of decoding the words on the page.

Readers' theater is not only an excellent way to increase fluency but also a good way to have fun while reading and build reading confidence. A helpful way to teach this is to provide passages for students to "polish" and then present orally for feedback on their delivery. An engaging way to do this is by asking students to practice appropriate readers' theater texts and reminding them to think about how a real person would actually "say" the lines they deliver as they read.

In addition to rereading, another helpful technique for building the skills of struggling readers is to pair them up with younger students as "reading buddies." Both students benefit when older children can read less challenging materials, such as picture books, to younger students. The younger child benefits by being read to, and the older student benefits by being able to have extensive practice with less-dense text than they might have to read at their own grade level. If done several times per week, skills continue to build for the reader and the younger student they are helping,

While fluency is often taught through activities where students read aloud, teachers must not forget that oral reading is a different skill than silent reading. As adults, we are more often called upon to read silently than we are to read orally. At this level, oral practice allows the teacher to hear the areas where the student is still struggling and provide the proper support the reader needs to improve their performance. Since most children are still not proficient silent readers, oral reading practice helps build solid skills that can transfer to silent reading.

While talking about oral reading, it is essential to talk about an ineffective practice that has long been used in classrooms, called "round robin" reading or "popcorn" reading. This is where students are asked to read a portion of text either in sequence as the teacher goes from student to student around the room or by reading when the teacher selects random students to continue reading where the last student left off.

If we ask adults what their most stressful school memory has been, most adults cite having to read orally in class as one of their most negative and stressful experiences. Since no child wants to look "dumb" in front of their peers, most of us practiced the survival skill of counting the paragraphs until we determined the one that would be assigned to us to read. We then silently read and reread that paragraph until it came time for us to deliver our part as fluently and skillfully as possible.

While we were busy practicing our part, we did not listen to the other students before ass they read their passages. Most of us were tied up in knots, worrying about the performance we would have to give in the next few minutes. After our reading, we were so happy to be finished that we seldom paid attention to those reading immediately after us either.

If a teacher thinks this is an effective instructional technique to help students improve oral reading, they are sadly mistaken. Instead, it is a good way to instill fear and dread in even the most capable readers. For this reason, round-robin reading is ineffective. Popcorn reading, where the teacher randomly calls on students to continue reading orally, is even worse for instilling effective reading habits. In this case, the student has lost the ability to practice the material ahead of time and sits in fear, dreading being called upon to read in front of their peers.

A better strategy to promote reading confidence and fluency is to allow students to practice oral reading with partners or a small group. With this approach, the fear factor has been eliminated from reading aloud in front of peers. Students can focus on listening and delivering a polished and confident oral delivery.

Another way to build fluency is finding fun passages to read in an echoing format. The teacher reads and models a sentence or two with good expression and prosody in echo reading. Then the students echo this reading in unison using the same expression and prosody. Some of Shel Silverstein's humorous poems are fun and engaging choices for echo reading practice. Since all students are actively reading during echo reading, there is no pressure on individual students. This is a perfect technique to use when many readers are struggling with fluency. It is also an excellent instructional strategy for English language learners.

Another excellent method of helping students develop oral fluency is choral reading. Choral reading is where groups of students read different parts of a poem or passage. The more students are allowed to practice a given text, the more smoothly and fluently they can deliver the message. This is also a good technique for readers who are not yet proficient or learning English.

Fun poems and text with refrains are good resources for practicing choral reading. Unlike the stressful "popcorn" or "round robin" reading of the past, children will enjoy participating in these kinds of activities. Students will develop stronger oral reading skills.

Students who struggle with reading may also be helped by listening to audio recordings via headsets and following along with the printed text. As they become more practiced, they can try to emulate the speaker's expression and reading fluency. Struggling readers may also benefit by listening to books on CD that they might never get through on their own. While this technique does not replace actual reading practice, it can increase vocabulary and background knowledge in students who lack these skills. Be sure to choose books that match the reader's interests and age level.

As students become fluent readers, we must also help them increase their reading rate. The eyes can quickly transmit large quantities of data to the brain, so we should take advantage of that ability. When we read faster, we become less "bogged down" with the process and can enjoy the content more.

We want children to learn to read quickly and efficiently so that reading is not a laborious and challenging task. To help children do this, we ask them to read the material at their independent reading level, and we time them while they read.

Children circle the last word read at the end of the allotted time, such as one minute. Each time they read a new passage we ask them to try to read the material more quickly than they did the time before. The number of words read divided by the number of minutes is the words per minute the child can read.

When students finish the passage, they are asked to answer comprehension questions to ensure they are decoding and comprehending the text. Over time and with practice, the reading rate will improve as students continue their work in this area. If they still have 90% accuracy or better, they are within expectations for maintaining accuracy while stretching to read faster.

Another problem children may have when learning to read is using sub-vocalization. When primary students begin to read, they often need to read out loud to understand what has been read. Around late first grade or early second grade, students are expected to transition from oral reading to silent reading.

When reading material at an independent reading level, the brain can process text without the child saying the words in their head or whispering them under their breath. Primary teachers report that many children have difficulty making this transition. Some children must be reminded to "Read in your head – not out loud." Telling students to read in their heads can lead to a different type of problem.

To avoid being corrected by the teacher, some children stop vocalizing out loud and change to allowing their brains to say the word in their heads while reading. Since the eyes and the brain can read much faster than words can be vocalized orally or in the brain, this subvocalization limits an individual's reading rate. This practice may continue into adulthood, causing adult readers to continue to read slowly.

Teach children to look at several words to improve their reading rate. This can be done by placing a text mask with a window cut out over the text and moving it back and forth across the page or by placing a finger down the center of the text and then "flashing the eyes" first on the left and then on the right of where the finger has been placed.

Quick comprehension checks ensure that the student maintains comprehension during the practice session. If comprehension is under 90 percent proficient, reduce the level of the practice text being used with the student. This, too, can help students effectively increase their reading rate.

Fluency is the rock foundation upon which good comprehension and higher-order thinking are built. The more a student has an opportunity to practice, the more capable a reader they will become. Building strong and fluent readers with good comprehension skills is the most critical goal for literacy instruction during the fourth and fifth grades. If students in grades 6-8 still have not developed solid oral fluency and a reasonable reading pace, it is absolutely essential that the teacher routinely use the strategies described in this section to strengthen these skills.

Before Reading Preparation

To be effective readers, students must understand that reading and thinking go hand in hand. From fourth grade on, we must help students understand that thinking and making meaning of what is being read is the essence of reading.

Students must have two sets of skills to be strong and capable readers. The first is metacognitive skills that allow the student to think about the meaning of their reading, and the second is mechanical skills that allow readers to process what they are reading. Metacognitive skills allow the reader to link their past experience to the new information and reflect on the meaning of the text. Mechanical skills allow readers to predict text properties and its organization. Students must actively engage in "doing" reading and thinking about their thoughts as they read.

Before reading, students must activate prior knowledge, make predictions, explore new vocabulary or concepts, and understand what they are supposed to get from the reading they are about to do. Teachers must carefully plan experiences that give students solid pre-reading direction and support.

Making Predictions and Activating Background Knowledge

Any time we pick up a book, we use prediction skills. We predict what a book will be about based on the title, the pictures, the front cover, the author, and information on the jacket or book back. From this information, we predict the content, our interest in the material, and our desire to read the book. We decide to read a particular book because we have established a purpose. The purpose may be to learn something new, understand a new idea, enjoy a story, or read about an engaging topic.

As adult readers, we often use predictive skills when we read. However, students may not understand how to use evaluative and predictive skills when reading.

Many choose a book to read because it is the smallest book on the shelf or the one with the most pictures. They may not understand that it is essential to select a book that matches one's interests, prior knowledge, background, or even reading ability. Talking to our students about our own thinking processes when selecting a book can help students understand how competent readers choose appropriate reading materials.

The way to build strong readers is by getting them to read about what interests or connects with them. We know that when readers are interested in a topic, reading motivation is increased. Students may even push themselves through more complex material when they can connect with the book's topic.

While encouraging students to read the things that interest them is excellent for encouraging independent reading, students are expected to read many texts in grades 4-12 that may not match their interests or background knowledge.

Helping students connect to texts that they may not have self-selected is essential. Pre-reading activities can help teachers increase student interest by activating background knowledge before reading a text. When students know the purpose, they are trying to accomplish and have reflected on what they know about the topic, students are more prepared to link what they already know about a topic to new ideas and concepts they will learn.

In addition to connecting with a text, students should also know in advance why they will be reading a specific text. What is the purpose of reading this text? Is the reading for personal pleasure? Will the information be used to answer questions? Will students complete a graphic organizer, write a summary of the key points, or analyze the author's point of view? When students understand the expected outcome, they can better understand the reading processes necessary to achieve their goal.

Before beginning any reading assignment, teachers must set the stage for students by helping them connect what they already know about a topic. Research shows that students learn more and retain more of their learning when the teacher first takes time to activate their prior knowledge around a subject (Beyer, 1991).

Teachers can activate prior knowledge using classroom discussions, graphic organizers, KWL charts, ABC brainstorming, word associations, study guides, or other fun techniques, such as word splashes, anticipation guides, or probable passage strategies.

In the following pages, you will find several strategies teachers may find helpful for activating background knowledge before reading. For in-depth descriptions of these techniques and many other ways to help students connect with their background knowledge, please see *Literacy Strategies for Grades 4-12: Reinforcing the Threads of Reading* (Tankersley, 2005).

You may also want to read the chapters on primary and high school reading since you will probably be working with students with a wide range of reading abilities, both below and above, in the classrooms where you will provide literacy coaching.

The more students connect with a text before reading, the more effective they will be at understanding the ideas and information they are learning. Therefore, teachers must help students activate prior learning before introducing new information. Here are some additional ways to help students connect with text.

Predicting Passage Content

Select ten to fifteen vocabulary words that are typical of the content in the passage and present them to students. Provide students with the story structure frame and ask them to predict which words belong to which story elements. Words representing the story elements should be selected, such as the character, setting, problem, etc. After students have read the story, have them compare their predictions and make changes as necessary. Use the corrected story elements organizer to summarize or retell the story.

Mind mapping

Before beginning the lesson, students are asked to brainstorm everything they know about a topic in word web form. After instruction, students review their web maps to determine any additional information that needs to be added or corrections that might need to be made. The central idea of this strategy is to help students compare background knowledge on the topic with new learning.

Promising Predictions

Write down the title and subtitles of a passage. Give students the text title and then have them write down what they think the text will be about based on the title. Then give the other text subtitles or headings one at a time, each time asking students to again consider the information and revise or add to their predictions of what they think the text will be about. Once students have made their predictions, ask them to read and compare the article to see how accurate they were in predicting the information they read in the text.

Get One and Give One

Ask students to write five to ten things they know about a topic on one side of their paper. Allow students to roam the class for two to three minutes, talking with other students and comparing lists. On the back side of the paper, each student writes one bit of information they did not have on their own list as the "get one" and then "gives one" to the other student to add to their own list. A fact can only be given one time.

As students record the information, they also record the name of the person who gave them the information next to the newly added fact. Students continue matching up with other students and getting and giving some information until the teacher calls time. Students then return to their seats and review their information on both sides of the paper. Students are then asked if they have questions about any of the information they have on their paper. Students are asked to read the text, verify the information, and modify any incorrect information. Follow-up discussions should then take place on what has been read.

Story Impressions

The teacher selects several words representative of the story's gist and provides these to the students before reading. The students are asked to examine the words, consider their implications, and construct a summary paragraph that they believe will match the text. Once the text has been read, students match their version with the original to see how well they predicted the story content.

KWL

While most teachers have heard about Know-Want to Know - Learned (KWL) charts, many do not know how to use them effectively to help students activate their background knowledge and construct meaningful questions about the topic to be studied. As a result, they often do not use them as tools to help students connect with what they already know about a topic. KWL charts are great introductions for new units. They can build student interest and motivation before reading. They can help teachers create excitement in a new unit topic. If you do not see teachers you work with, occasionally use this valuable tool, demonstrate how to use it effectively as a unit introduction.

During-Reading Strategies

As was said earlier, reading is a participation sport, and you must *read* to become an effective reader. Students must be engaged in reading more than talking about reading or doing worksheets about reading skills. Skill sheets, or "drill and kill," do not directly build strong readers any more than doing worksheets about swimming or golfing would build strong athletes.

Teachers must deliberately plan how students will engage in the actual reading part of the lesson. If students have difficulty staying engaged, begin with reading tasks that last no more than ten minutes at a time. As students gain increased stamina and fluency, slowly increase the reading tasks to twenty or even thirty minutes at a time. Again, the more students engage in reading, the more proficient they will become.

Poor readers often think that teachers are masters of all types of reading and that we never struggle with reading tasks. They think good readers are never confused. Students, particularly those who struggle with reading, are quick to cover their confusion when trying to understand the text. To build confidence in readers, we must create a safe and secure environment where students feel they can take risks and verbalize their questions and confusion as they read.

We must let students know that no matter how proficient the reader is, there are texts which can present difficulty to even the most proficient reader. For example, how well did you understand the mortgage contract you were asked to sign or the credit card revision statement sent to you the last time the credit card company made revisions to your terms of service? Unless you have some background knowledge of the law or legal documents, you were most likely challenged when reading these texts. That is because most of us do not have the background knowledge to understand this type of text. Background knowledge helps us understand while we are reading.

We would learn to understand these documents' jargon and writing styles over time with repeated practice. As a result, our proficiency would grow. However, as "novice" readers, individuals have not developed the proper background knowledge and skill to effectively and confidently process these documents.

Metacognition: Thinking About Our Thinking

Helping students understand that we all have difficulty and lose meaning from time to time helps students have more confidence to ask questions and use fix-up strategies when they recognize that meaning has been lost. We can help students develop this understanding by modeling our thinking process as we read so that we can open a window on how proficient readers think as they process a text. The more students actively engage in reading, the better readers students will become.

To help students "think about their own thinking," we need to help them understand when their understanding of what they are reading breaks down. We then need to give students ways to get back on track when they get distracted, lose their place, or realize they do not understand what they are reading.

Students need to identify where understanding broke down, or they lost connection with the text. Then we need to help them understand how to get back on track so that the text has meaning.

We can help students by acknowledging when they have "unglued" from the text and showing them how to refocus themselves on the text they need to read. If the text has been unclear, we can help them understand that some strategies they can use are:

1) keep reading to see if the passage gets more transparent as they read more of the text;

2) go back and reread the unclear part from a sentence or two before where meaning was lost;

3) slow down the reading rate or read the text aloud to see if it becomes more apparent;

4) try to connect the unclear part to something you already know about;

5) try to chunk the sentences into phrases to see what you need help understanding;

6) discuss the unclear part with a friend or adult (if available) or make a note to ask someone for help clarifying the idea in the text later and continue reading.

Students must also be taught the skills of predicting, visualizing, and making connections. With fiction, students should predict what a text will likely be about, what will happen, and how characters might respond, solve problems, or handle conflicts in fiction stories.

In nonfiction, they should predict what information they will learn and how it might relate to their questions about the topic being discussed. Students should be asked to describe what they picture characters or scenes to be like or how they view the action or scene in the text.

In fiction and nonfiction, helping students connect the new information and what they already know about the situation or concept is vital to good comprehension. Graphic organizers can help students visualize the relationships or parts of a process about which they are reading in the text. We can help them do this by asking them to identify what it reminds them of or what they have learned or experienced that is similar. When students make solid connections to the text, comprehension increases, and retention is better.

Partner Reading

Partner reading for students in grades 4-8 is an effective way to read. There are two types of partner reading: shared reading, where students take turns reading aloud, and silent reading, where students read silently and then discuss the text content at key stopping points in the text. For older readers, teachers should give partner pairs the choice of whether they wish to read orally or silently.

Readers who struggle with the text and English language learners often prefer to read aloud since this may help them comprehend the material more easily. Fluent readers, on the other hand, may choose to read silently because it's quicker and more efficient for them. Teachers might consider providing students with sticky notes to insert into the text whenever they find a confusing point or want to ask a clarifying question to their partner about something in the text.

Small Group Reading

In addition to partner reading, the teacher may also want to occasionally use small-group reading with groups of three or four students sharing the reading task either silently or orally, as described earlier. Allow students to choose the method of reading that works best for most readers in the group. Keep ability levels mixed to support each group's struggling or English language learners more effectively.

For older readers, ask each student to become an "expert" on a particular section of the text and then explain it to their group members so that everyone understands the text well. Groups of students, particularly with content texts, might also be given a particular section of text to read and discuss. Following the discussion, each group is asked to create and give a short presentation to the class on the key points they learned in that section of the text. Here are several other effective techniques to use during reading.

Who Can Summarize?

The teacher reads a selection of text to the students and asks students to follow along silently. At critical points in the text, the teacher asks the class, "Who can summarize what we have just heard?" Students then volunteer to summarize the key points from the text passage. The teacher may ask other students to contribute any additional details or information that may have been missed.

The teacher can also take this opportunity to ask prediction or anticipation-type questions for what may come in subsequent pages. With the teacher reading the text, all class members hear the text, and no one is concerned about counting passages to pre-read the text or that they might be called upon to read orally. This technique works well for fiction and nonfiction texts and improves comprehension for all students.

Reflecting and Retelling

Encourage students to pause after each chapter, once or twice during a picture book, and after each textbook section. Model aloud how you stop, think, and then retell to monitor how much you recall from the text. Point out that thinking and retelling reinforce retention of the text. If there is little recall, then reread and try to retell again.

Students can also write down the retelling in their reading notebooks. Once you have modeled the strategy, read a passage to the students and stop at strategic points. Ask students to retell what has been read as you have modeled. Practice this strategy until all students can retell the section of text they have been asked to summarize during their turn reasonably accurately.

Metacognitive Reading Reflections

If you want students to really think about how they are reading, help them monitor the strategies they are applying during reading. Examine how they connect with the text. Evaluate the successes and confusions they have encountered.

In a spiral binder, have students record the date, the text being read, the beginning and ending page numbers and the time spent reading during that session. Write sentence stems such as: "I got confused when..."; "I was distracted when..."; "I got myself back on track when..."; "I stopped reading when..."; "I figured out that..." and similar starting stems on the board. Ask students to choose one or more to respond to in their spiral binder for that time. Teachers may want to occasionally gather up the logs and read and respond to student reflections about their own reading growth, successes, and challenges.

Shared Text Exploration

Begin by placing students in small groups of similar ability levels. Using an appropriate graphic organizer for story structure, assign each group two or three boxes to complete. Teachers can also ask students to look for specific features while reading a text. For example, a more struggling group might be asked to locate the author and setting.

Another group might be asked to identify the characters and the central problem the main character faces, and so forth. Advanced students might be asked to write a summary statement about the story. Other advanced groups might be asked to compare and contrast the story with others like it or events. When each group has completed their part of the project, hold a class discussion over the material.

Prediction Signals

Another helpful skill for students is identifying authors' signal words in the text. Signal words help readers understand and predict what information will be presented in the text. For example, when the author includes a question in the text, the author will most likely go on to answer that question in the paragraphs which follow the question.

When readers come across a colon in text, they can most likely expect that the author will follow with a list of items that are examples. Sometimes groups of words such as "in other words," "means," or "is equal to" signal the reader that they will find a definition of a new term or concept in the text which follows. By explicitly helping students understand signal words in a text, we can better prepare them to predict the content they may see in their reading text.

Clarifying and Visualizing

In this strategy, students are told by the teacher to put a flag post at specific stopping points in the text they will be reading. Students then read the passage silently with a partner. When both readers come to the flag in the text, each person stops and answers the five W (who, what, where, when, why) and How questions about the text. They then create a picture in their mind (or on paper) of what they think the passage means and what is happening in this section of the text. The pair then discusses their pictures and impressions of what has happened in this text section. This summarizing technique, along with the visualization strategy, helps students clarify their understanding of the material and allows readers to practice visualizing the meaning of text.

After-Reading Strategies

After reading a text, we want students to think about and reflect on what they have read. Students must learn to make connections between the text and their own lives (text-to-self connections), draw comparisons between various texts they have read (text-to-text connections), and make connections between text and their knowledge of the world (text-to-world connections). After-reading activities allow students to process at higher thinking levels and cement what they have learned by connecting it to their prior knowledge.

Some ways to do this include having students present a lesson to their peers about what they have learned, design a project to illustrate their information, create a debate, act out the information, or write about it. Students may also complete graphic organizers, compare pre-reading predictions to the actual text, or journal about the information they have learned. Technology can also be used to explore more information about the topic or compare what they have read to other sources. Here are some fun ways to help students summarize and think about what they have read.

ABC Topic Books

Creating ABC topic books is a fun and effective technique to summarize what students have learned from their reading. After students have studied a topic, assign one sub-area of the topic to each group. For example, if the broad topic was pollution, groups could take various components of this topic, such as water pollution, air pollution, light pollution, ground contamination, etc. Students would research their topic and brainstorm important words for each letter from A to Z. They would then create a sentence and illustrated page for each letter of the alphabet explaining their topic. The pages could be spiral bound and then given to younger students to enjoy or kept in the room for students to read and re-read.

Asking Questions – Giving Answers

After students have read their assigned text in a small group or partner format, ask them to develop a specific number of questions about the text and the answers. Tell students that the questions should be solid "right there—in the text" questions that can easily be verified in the text. They should be main-idea questions and not obscure points to trick another group with comprehension.

Once each group has completed their questions, have them exchange question sets with another group, discuss the questions, and record their responses. The responses are then returned to the first group, where the scores of the responses are checked for accuracy. If the class has difficulty creating meaningful and appropriate questions, give points for the number right the other team gets on their responses. This will encourage students to give meaningful and quickly answered sets of comprehension questions to the other team.

QAR

A more advanced form of question-and-answer is the Question-Answer Relationship strategy (Raphael et al., 2006), known as QARs. Raphael says that there are two types of QAR questions. The answers to "in the book" and "in my head" questions are not explicitly stated and must be inferred from the text.

In this strategy, students are asked to develop questions using Raphael's four types of questions: "Right There, Think and Search, Author and Me, and On My Own." Each question requires students to have a different level of understanding as they attempt to create a question or answer it based on the text they read. Questions known as "right there" are detailed types of questions where the words used to form the question can be found "right there" in the text.

Think and Search questions can be found in the text, but readers have to "think and search" to find the answer sometimes in more than one place in the text. For the Author and Me types of questions, the answer comes from the reader's background knowledge and the information gained from the text.

The final type of question is the On My Own type of question. These questions relate to the text but could probably be answered even without a reader ever having read the text. The ideas and information for responding to the question come entirely from the reader's background knowledge.

Questions that students generate about a text can be answered in small groups or asked in a whole class setting. Students can be called upon by the teacher or their peers to respond to various questions, or class members can volunteer to respond if they wish. As students become more proficient at creating the four question types, ask them to also tell students the type of question they have created before asking others to answer it.

Sentence Strip Organization

Here is another way to help students think about what they have read. The teacher cuts the text of a story into individual sentences and places the sentence strips into an envelope with one set per group of students. Students work in groups to examine and reassemble the various sentences into a reasonable sequence. Each group reads their story aloud, and then the teacher reads the original printed text for comparison. Students discuss the clues they used to order the story strips into the sequence the group chose for their versions.

Writing What We Heard

With students organized in small groups of similar ability, provide a passage of an appropriate reading level. Choose one student to read the material entirely, or have a couple of students take turns reading aloud if the text is long. While the story is being read, the rest of the group members listen attentively or actively take notes. When the reading is completed, students write a summary of what they read. Students can later share their text summaries with the class if the teacher desires.

Teaching Students to Summarize Text

Although teachers often ask students to create summaries, they often do not know how to create a summary of a text they have just read. Begin explicitly teaching students this essential skill by providing a short passage on an overhead or document camera. First, read the passage to the students in its entirety. Then begin again and think aloud as you examine the paragraphs for the main idea of the paragraph and key details.

Continue helping students "think through" summary creation until they have completed an appropriate summarization of the article. Once you have demonstrated how to think through the passage, cover or remove the passage and ask students to help you reflect on the article's main point as you write the summary on another overhead transparency, document or the whiteboard. If students need to refresh the information for an idea or two from the paragraph, reshow the original text so that students can locate any key information that everyone agrees belongs in the summary paragraph.

Practice several more times as a whole group activity similarly until most students can easily identify what information should become part of the summary. Then allow students to do the same in small groups and later on their own as they refine their ability to accurately and succinctly create text summaries. As students become more proficient, have them trade summaries and provide feedback to their peers. Teachers can also have students read their summaries aloud and discuss which summaries seem most effective at communicating the text's key points.

Differentiating Reading Abilities in the Classroom

The Internet makes it easy to locate materials at various reading levels on the same topic for classroom content use. Many publishers now offer specialized materials written for a high-interest and low vocabulary or English language learner needs. You can even find magazines for use in the classroom that are differentiated.

For example, *National Geographic* publishes magazines coded in the upper left corner for beginner, middle, and advanced readers. Publishers also sell topic-specific books which are coded for different reading levels. Teachers can also download material from the Internet on the same topic to provide content for various reading levels in the classroom.

Place students into groups and have them work on group projects appropriate to their development and skill level. These are helpful ways that teachers can provide for the diverse backgrounds and skill levels seen in classrooms nationwide.

Vocabulary Strategies

Children learn vocabulary both explicitly through deliberate classroom instruction, where we explain the meaning of various words to them, and indirectly through everyday experiences. We learn words all of our lives indirectly when we see or hear words in different contexts. This can be through listening to conversations, being read to, or reading and seeing words in context while reading.

Word meanings can also be explicitly taught to us, such as when we are told the meaning of a new word, when we look a word up in a reference book, or when we ask someone directly the meaning of a new word. We have an oral vocabulary, a reading vocabulary, and a vocabulary we use in writing.

Each individual has a receptive vocabulary: words we recognize when we hear or see them. We also have a productive vocabulary that we use when we speak or write. The receptive vocabulary is usually more extensive since people often recognize more words even if they don't know their complete definitions and connotations or use them when they speak or write.

According to researchers Baumann, Kameenui, and Ash (2003), the extent of a student's vocabulary knowledge is strongly related to their reading comprehension and overall academic success. Students must have many words in their knowledge storehouse and good strategies to use when encountering new words they don't recognize.

When students have a specific word in their oral vocabulary, they can more easily recognize these words while reading. For this reason, it is essential that teachers systematically spend a substantial amount of time helping students acquire new words in both their receptive and productive vocabularies.

Before reading, teachers should explicitly teach words vital to comprehend the material being read so that students will recognize these words when they come to them. We should also explicitly teach words that the student will likely see often in the material being studied.

Previewing important terms is particularly important for content area lessons where there are many words that students are not likely to already have in their working vocabularies. Teachers should be sure to teach scientific or specialized terms that students will need to comprehend the subject matter being read.

Other words that should be explicitly taught are words that have multiple meanings. Students may know the word in one context but not in the other contexts. For example, "bank" could be both a noun and a verb. The word as a noun could refer to an institution where one conducts financial transactions; the slope on the side of a body of water; a row of objects; or even a pile of snow. The word can also be used as a verb, as in "The airplane banked left" or "The man banked the ball into the right pool table pocket." It's no wonder that even native-born children have trouble with the English language, much less English language learners trying to learn this complex language.

Researchers Robbins and Ehri (1994) concluded that vocabulary instruction methods where students are given the definition of the word, examples of usage of the word, and practice with using the word have produced the most significant gains in retention and comprehension.

Several studies have verified that activities such as semantic webs, word maps, and graphic organizers, where students can graphically depict the word and its meaning and identify pictorial connections to the meaning of the word, are effective instructional strategies for vocabulary learning. What is not an effective instructional strategy for vocabulary learning is the old practice of "assign, define, and test" used in many classrooms to teach vocabulary.

Word Walls, Affixes, and Word Origins

Although many primary teachers actively use word walls, teachers in grades 4-8 should also have word walls. These word walls should feature language students need unique to the disciplines being studied. Learning words requires many exposures over time for the word and its associated meanings to become easily accessible to students. Word walls might contain word families with similar prefixes or suffixes, such as biology, zoology, and graphology.

Teaching prefixes, suffixes, and root words and their related meanings to students helps unlock new vocabulary terms. Teaching students to break apart words into their prefixes, root words, and suffixed elements is an effective strategy to unlock word meaning. Learning the origin of words helps students predict spelling patterns and meaning.

Vocabulary Fish

Identify about ten sets of four words that belong to the same family group. Write these words on three-by-five-inch cards to have approximately fifty cards per set. Students can then play a game similar to the card game Fish. To begin the game, the first player calls another player by name and requests a card of a specific type. For example, player one may ask player two if he has any cards with the names of a family member on them, such as "aunt," "sister," "brother," "mother," and so forth. If player two holds such a card, he gives the card to player one and draws another card from the face-down deck. He can lay down a matching set when player one has acquired four cards.

If player two does not hold a card from this word family in his hand, he tells player one to "Go fish!" Player one then does this by drawing a card from the face-down deck, and his turn is over.

Player one may continue to ask other players for cards as long as he receives a card from each player or until he has completed a matching set of four cards.

Vocabulary Gotcha!

To create this game, you can use a list of antonyms, synonyms, or words and their matching definitions. Place the linking words on blank three-by-five-inch cards so you have approximately fifty cards. Create one card for the deck with "Gotcha!" written.

This game is similar to the classic card game "Old Maid" and is played similarly. All cards are dealt out to the players. The players first look at their cards and discard any matching pairs. Play is clockwise.

At each turn, the player offers his cards to the player on his left. The player on the left selects a card from the offering player's hand without seeing it and adds the card to his own collection of cards. If the card creates a pair, player two matches the cards and discards the pair into his discard pile. The player who just took the new card then offers his hand to the next player and repeats the process until all players have had a chance to choose a card, match cards if possible, and create discards. If the player does not have a match for the card drawn, the card is added to the player's hand, where it stays until drawn by another player or matched.

Eventually, all cards will be matched and discarded except for the Gotcha! card. The person who ends up with the Gotcha! card is considered the game's good-natured loser, which was "gotten."

Inspiring Words

Give the class a small passage that is missing words. Each student will then complete the passage with words he thinks will make the passage more interesting. After the class completes the passage, have each student share their passage to see who can create the most descriptive and interesting passage.

Roll a Word

A student rolls six letter cubes in a cup. The student uses the letters rolled to create words consisting of two to six letters. Words are recorded on a recording sheet, with one point being given for each letter contained in the word. An egg timer may be used to monitor each student's thinking time as they examine the letters rolled from their toss. The total number of letters equals the score, with the person with the highest score at the end of play being declared the game-winner.

What's My Category?

Provide students with sets of words from the same category. Students will examine the word sets and identify which word is the category. For example, if the student were given "ocean," "lake," "water," and "bay" as words to categorize, the student would select "water" as the category.

Reducing Vocabulary Density

One way to assist ELL students or struggling readers is by reducing the vocabulary level in a text. To do this, place a transparency over a page of written material. Using a fine-point black marker, cross out the more difficult words and write simpler equivalents of these words above the more difficult word or in the text margins. As students read, they can substitute the easier words for the more difficult ones.

Technology

By grades 4-8, technology is necessary for every classroom, no matter what content is being taught. There are so many ways digital cameras, laptops, digital response systems, and online research can motivate learning and broaden student knowledge that teachers can no longer ignore technology as an effective and vital learning tool. Teachers must find ways to blend effective technology tools in their subject fields with day-to-day classroom learning.

Technology can help teachers provide for the many different learning styles in any classroom and help students learn to manage the vast amount of data that comes at them daily in meaningful and productive ways. Although many teachers are relatively proficient in using technology on a personal level, they don't always use technology in teaching-related tasks, such as student portfolios, tutorials, demonstrations, simulations, and student collaboration (Iding, Crosby & Speitel, 2002).

Students at this level can initiate and direct some of their own learning. They should be taught to share knowledge with one another, write to learn, and think critically about what they are learning. Students should use technology to write, create, and communicate with others.

An excellent example of how students can use technology to explore their creativity and build writing skills is by participating in online story development, as with the National Children's Book and Literacy Alliance's the Exquisite Corpse Adventure at https://www.thencbla.org/Exquisite_Corpse/exquisite_home.html

In this wonderful story, everyone shares in the mystery and excitement. The White House Project, also found on this site, would be an excellent addition to any social studies class in grades 4-8.

More learning occurs when students read, write, and explore purposefully.

Technology can significantly add interest and motivation for middle-grade students. Many students are quite adept at using technology such as smartphones, iPads, and computers, so the more teachers can capitalize on their natural talents, the more middle school students are likely to read when technology is brought into the mix. Literacy coaches can act as a conduit between teachers in the school for sharing and modeling effective technology strategies and techniques.

Conclusion

In this chapter, we have discussed what the classroom for students in grades 4-8 should look like and feel like, what instructional methods should be seen to support strong literacy learning, and how technology can play a role in helping teachers provide for the many needs of students at this age level. The research on what constitutes effective literacy instruction has never been more substantial, and the tools are readily available. Literacy coaches must help teachers explore and incorporate effective ways of building strong literacy skills in students daily.

In the resources section, you will find a survey on the classroom environment and instructional strategies for middle-grade classrooms. You can use these instruments to help intermediate teachers target areas they wish to work on with you during your coaching time.

Please provide a copy of the survey and ask teachers to privately rank their own proficiency in each area of reading instruction. Once they have done this, ask them to think about areas where they would like assistance, more information, or targeted coaching.

Once they have identified areas of interest, please discuss the areas of strength and where the teacher would like to expand their skills. Develop specific and measurable goals that you and your colleague can use to guide your work together.

"If teachers are to prepare an ever more diverse group of students for much more challenging work – for framing problems; finding, integrating and synthesizing information; creating new solutions; learning on their own; and working cooperatively – they will need substantially more knowledge and radically different skills than most now have, and most schools of education now develop."
Linda Darling-Hammond (1997, p. 154)

Chapter 3

Literacy Development for High School Teachers

♋

The Productive Literacy Learning Environment for High School Students

Whether students are going to college or into the workforce following high school, students must be able to read analytically and comprehend complex texts, write clearly and persuasively, and problem-solve regularly. For this reason, in successful high schools, all teachers, no matter what discipline they teach, understand and accept that they must not only teach their specific content but also teach students to read, write, and think logically in that discipline. When high school teachers embrace this responsibility, the classroom and school atmosphere support strong literacy development.

What Does Effective Reading Instruction
Look Like in Grades 9-12?

In a classroom that supports strong literacy development, the approach to reading will look different from that of the traditional classroom. In the old content instruction paradigm, teachers typically gave an assignment. They asked students to read independently or led an in-class group reading of the text, often in round-robin fashion. Sometimes students were asked to respond to chapter questions provided by the publisher on text content. After the reading, a teacher-led discussion occurred over the material to see if the students understood the content. Then, students were tested over the chapter's material to determine understanding.

While successful readers did, in fact, learn from this approach, many students, particularly the less-capable readers, did not benefit from this type of instructional approach. Often less-capable students either tuned out or acted out and learned primarily from the teacher-led discussions and/or in-class activities rather than from the text material they were supposed to read and process. Student content knowledge was minimal, and teachers lamented that their students weren't successful because they couldn't read the textbooks they had been given.

While teachers clearly understand that their students aren't able to read and can't access their dense textbooks, many content teachers do not know what to do about the situation. While they have been well trained in their content discipline, most have not had much, if any, training in how to help students read or process concept-dense text such as that found in most content textbooks. For this reason, literacy coaches must help content teachers shift their instructional paradigm to a more effective paradigm which includes a better understanding of the reading process and how active readers process and connect with text on deep and meaningful levels.

To understand how successful reading instruction might look at the high school level, let's spend some time visiting several successful high school classrooms.

Visiting Vince – Ninth Grade Science

The first classroom we will visit is that of ninth-grade science teacher Vince. Vince has been teaching for over twenty years. Just in the past five years, as his school implemented reading across the curriculum strategies in all content classrooms, he has felt he has become skilled at helping his students grow in their reading and understanding of science.

As we enter the classroom, we see a large bulletin board area where words such as "biosphere," "lithosphere," "cryosphere," "atmosphere," "sedimentation," "metamorphism," "orogenesis," and "geochemical" have been placed. Pictures, word origins and definitions next to each word help students remember the meaning of these scientific words.

On another wall, we see posters of soil and land erosion and steps that environmentalists are taking to combat this erosion in various topographies around the world. On another wall, we see several graded student reports about water reclamation efforts in various parts of the world, complete with pictures and graphs in each report.

Vince tells us that the class has been working on learning about geochemical cycles for the past couple of weeks. He points to the reports that students recently completed on water reclamation. He tells us that students work in teams of five and study the various geochemical cycles, such as carbon, water, and rock. Vince has written several higher-level questions to students on the reports at various points to stimulate students' thinking about the water reclamation efforts they discussed.

We see some students creating flow charts and others using classroom netbooks to research their topics on the Internet. As they review different websites, the students note who is sponsoring the Web site and discuss the probable reliability of the information they are finding. They also use lateral reading techniques to check out what other information they can find about the reliability of the website hosts. Occasionally, Vince's students print out sections of the information when it appears helpful to their understanding of the cycle they are studying.

Other students read, discuss, and take notes from their textbooks, reference books, and government pamphlets Vince provided. As students read to their partners, they discuss the material and decide how to summarize their information in note form on their yellow tablets. We hear them ask one another, "Does this seem right?" and "What do you think this means?" as group members read and re-read the material to gain additional information and text clarity.

All students are on task and highly engaged in their respective tasks. Vince says that each group will construct a visual to represent the information they have found on their assigned topic. They will also make an oral presentation to the class two days from now. He laughs and says that from past experience, his students know he will hold firm on this deadline. This has pressured students to ensure they have well-prepared presentations for their peers by the due date.

Vince tells us that his students have gained a deeper knowledge of their topics since using this approach to learning science. Another benefit is that they clearly enjoy learning more. As the bell rings, he reminds a couple of deeply engrossed students that they must pack up and move on to their next class. He smiles at us and winks as we move out of the room and head down the hallway to our next high school classroom.

Visiting Samantha – Tenth Grade – Social Studies: World History

Next, we enter Samantha's 10th-grade world history classroom. Samantha has been teaching social studies for ten years. She loves teaching Social Studies and is active in the state chapter of the National Council for Social Studies. Since she has been networking with social studies teachers from around the state and attending conferences on effective social studies teaching, she says that her instructional repertoire has grown tremendously.

As we enter the room, we see a bulletin board with current events clippings and the faces of several world leaders with their names and countries below. We see several student-developed charts posted around the room with various graphic organizers on topics students have recently been studying in Samantha's class.

On a work counter in the classroom, we see neat tubs of Scholastic *New York Times Upfront* current events magazines and stacks of newspapers that appear to be well-used by students. We also see stacks of spiral-bound notebooks labeled "Social Studies Reflection Journals." The notebooks are organized by class period in other plastic tubs.

A box with iPads neatly packed inside is also on the counter and available for student use. On another wall, we see lists of prefixes, suffixes, and root words commonly used in social studies. There is also a small word wall with some specialized terms that Samantha wants students to know and be able to use during this unit of study.

On a bookshelf, we see many biographies and books related to the various social studies content topics Samantha teaches during the year. An extensive set of wall maps and a globe are near the front of the room. Several other graphs and charts are posted in strategic locations around the room.

Students are in groups of four with their desks facing together. Walking around, each group studies a different area, including Armenia, Cambodia, Bosnia, Nazi Germany, Rwanda, Kosovo, and Sudan. They read materials about various parts of the world where extreme nationalism has resulted in genocide.

One student uses the class textbook; others have selected articles and books from a stack of other materials Samantha provided to explore their assigned area. As students read the material, they take notes. Their record sheet has a place for recording the information source at the top and two columns. The left column has the heading "What the Text Says," while the right column is labeled "What It Means."
Students are busily reading and recording information on both sides of the text.

Occasionally, students read passages from their materials to other group members and ask for help clarifying the information they have read to check for understanding. Other group members are very willing to stop and listen and offer advice on interpreting the information to their group members. After the temporary assistance, group members work on their texts and recording sheets.

Samantha says that following each group's research, the class will discuss their findings and organize the information into a class compare/contrast chart. This, she says, will help students summarize and have greater insight and understanding into what happened politically in each situation where genocide has occurred.

Students will then identify the common political situations and factors that lead to this outcome based on their study of real-life events where genocide occurred. Samantha tells us that during tomorrow's class, students will have a guest visitor from Bosnia to speak about fleeing Bosnia and what her family experienced as a result of the genocide taking place in her country. Students are excited about this visitor and eager to be well-prepared on the topic before her arrival.

We are impressed with how focused each group is on their reading and thank Samantha for letting us take a peek into her classroom. She smiles and tells us to stop back any time as we slip out the door and head off to the next high school classroom.

Visiting Gina – Junior English

On our last visit, we meet Gina, one of the Junior class English teachers. Gina loves literature and enjoys getting her students interested in reading about all types of literature, from classical to contemporary. She is well known on the staff as an excellent instructor who can develop students who love literature and become strong writers and thinkers. Our final classroom visit is to Gina's junior English class.

Gina's room contains several paperback book carousels filled with contemporary paperback novels. On one wall are student recommendations for books that other students might like to read.

Next to the recommendations area is a bulletin board where students have posted trite and over-used words on word cards around the words "R.I.P."

Student essays are posted on another bulletin board. The title of this board is "Making Connections and Reflecting on What We Have Read." several large pillows are propped up against the wall in the back corners of the room. Students can use these areas to enjoy a new book when they finish a classroom assignment.

We can see that students sit in three large circles in the classroom. Each group is busily discussing an assigned reading selection that Gina provided. One group discusses a reading selection from Robert Louis Stevenson's *Dr. Jekyll and Mr. Hyde*. Another group discusses a reading selection from H. G. Wells' *The Time Machine*. A third group discusses a reading selection from William Golding's *Lord of the Flies*.

Each group has a discussion moderator who asks the students probing questions from a list, such as: "What do we already know about the character of...?" "How does (concept) relate to what we have discussed in this book?" "Can you give me an example where..." and "Why do you suppose the author had character (name) ... (do or say a specific thing)?" The discussion easily comes from the students as they work through the moderator's open-ended questions for the text they have been assigned.

As students offer responses to the open-ended questions, other students from the group often challenge the speaker to provide a page and paragraph from the text reading that supports their comments, assertions, and opinions. We hear them ask, "Where in the text did you get this?" or "What page and paragraph are you reading from?" Gina circulates from group to group and makes notes. At the same time, she listens but only occasionally makes a comment to the group.

As the discussion continues, examples of the author's use of irony, plot, character contradictions, paradoxes, incongruities, and ambiguities from the story are discussed. As examples are identified, a group recorder makes a note on a sheet of chart paper where each example has been found in the text. The chart appears to be an ongoing activity that students use each time they discuss a new section of their text.

At the end of twenty minutes, Gina calls time and asks students to determine their next reading assignment. She explains that her literary discussion groups only take place every third day to allow all students to complete their reading and be prepared for the discussion groups.

When time is up, students return to their assigned areas and begin writing in a discussion reflection log. Gina explains that she asks students to record new connections they have made and new understandings about the text they are reading.

Gina says he periodically collects the reflective journals, reads them, and responds to the students. She also tells us this is a helpful way to assess her students' literary understanding and reading comprehension progress. Students say they enjoy it when she writes to them about the material. They also say their journals are an excellent place to privately ask Gina about confusing events or passages they didn't quite understand. They say that Gina always takes time to respond to them whenever they need more help or have questions about their learning. She is approachable and very knowledgeable about her content area.

We thank Gina for allowing us to observe her students and quietly slip out the classroom door.

Helping Students Comprehend Text

Research on appropriate instructional strategies suggests seven cognitive strategies that effective teachers should use to help students comprehend text content (Pearson et al., 1992).
These strategies are:

1) Activating background knowledge to make connections between new learning and prior information;

2) Questioning the text while reading;

3) Drawing inferences to make predictions;

4) Determining the importance of sorting through and prioritizing information;

5) Creating mental images and visualizing;

6) repairing understanding when meaning breaks down; and finally,

7) Synthesizing information to make meaning of the text and integrate their new understandings into their views. Effective content classrooms will use these strategies to help students better connect with and learn from text.

Literacy coaches must help content teachers learn the importance of front-loading instruction by spending time on pre-reading activities such as prediction, forming questions and establishing purpose for reading, clarifying new vocabulary, and brainstorming and activating prior knowledge about the topic so that new knowledge can be categorized and linked to existing knowledge. When teachers spend time helping students establish the foundation for new content, student motivation will improve, and student content understanding can also be taken to deeper levels.

The high school literacy coach can help content teachers assess the classroom literacy environment by examining the use of pre-reading activities regularly.

- How does the teacher activate prior knowledge and help students engage with key concepts before asking them to read?
- Do they provide focus and purpose for reading?
- Do they help students think about and form questions to guide the reading process?
- Do they build on the student's background knowledge to link new learning to what is already known?

By asking these questions, the literacy coach can help teachers identify areas to target for growth.

Literacy coaches should also see a strong emphasis on building vocabulary, concepts, and terminology in the content area. Literacy-supportive classrooms have word walls and/or word collection areas where new words are prominently featured. Students become word collectors; students and teachers are interested in words appropriate to the discipline. Word learning is clearly valued and encouraged in the class. Students study essential affixes and root words commonly used in the content area. They are introduced to strategies to deconstruct and reassemble words to determine meaning.

Once teachers prepare their students for reading content text, they must engage them in active reading. Active reading includes reading, interpreting, clarifying, and summarizing the content text.

During reading, students work with partners or in groups, share reading tasks, and discuss content with peers as needed to clarify meaning and understanding. There are periodic stopping points during the lesson to allow for summarizing of information, prediction checking, or asking clarifying questions.

Students are instructed to use appropriate "fix-up" strategies, such as looking back at the text, re-reading, and clarifying, to ensure comprehension and deep learning. Students are actively engaged in reading, thinking, and reflection about the lesson content and the information provided, with the high school teacher serving as a guide and facilitator of learning.

This might then be followed by post-reading activities designed to extend, clarify, and reinforce the learning that has taken place during the lesson. After reading, literacy coaches will see students applying the information in new and unique ways, such as participating in reflective and meaningful discussions, writing summaries, creating projects, completing graphic organizers, using role-play, or other active learning strategies to display their understanding.

Students will also be involved in clarifying concepts and understandings and connecting new knowledge to prior knowledge and other sources of information. The teacher directly teaches reading and writing strategy lessons that promote comprehension and content-specific reading strategies. The teacher takes time to read aloud to students in the content area and models "thinking aloud" about content regularly so that students hear how good readers process text in the content area. The teacher introduces various reading materials, such as articles and supplemental readings, to meet the needs of various reading abilities. The textbook is just one of many sources of information.

Here are some ideas to consider when evaluating a classroom literacy environment:

- •Does the classroom have a warm, positive, and supportive atmosphere in the room at all times?
- •Does the English classroom have a variety of different types and levels of books (i.e., fiction and nonfiction, high interest-low vocabulary, reference, audiobooks, magazines, comic books, online books) available to students? Is there an area where students can share book recommendations and reviews?
- •Does the content classroom have various books and articles (both traditional and contemporary) that align with instructional content topics and are written at various reading levels?
- •Are there print materials and images representative of the cultures and races of classroom populations visible in the room?
- •Does the teacher explore student interests and include a variety of resources beyond just the core textbook?
- •Is there abundant, high-quality student work posted on the classroom walls and bulletin boards?
- •Do both students and teacher appear to enjoy one another's company?
- • Do students appear willing to take risks and display relaxed self-confidence when approaching instructional tasks?

The coach will also want to help the teacher consider the instruction taking place in the classroom. The following questions can help:

- •Does the teacher help students reflect on their own reading habits and interests? Does the teacher provide opportunities for students to explore and grow as independent and capable readers?

- Does the teacher include a wide variety of text levels in the classroom?
- Does the content teacher use traditional or text-based readings, timely articles, and/or contemporary fiction when appropriate?
- Does the teacher thoughtfully organize lessons to include before-, during-, and after-reading goals and strategies?
- Does the teacher help students set purposeful content reading and learning goals?
- Does the teacher provide some choice in work projects and flexibly group and regroup students according to instructional needs?
- Does the teacher use appropriate assessments and regular observations to guide student needs and instructional practices?
- Does the teacher provide support to build student self-confidence and increase reading stamina and persistence?
- Do struggling readers have additional support within the classroom to help them close the gap between their current performance level and grade-level expectations? Does the school have Tier 2 and Tier 3 RtI support for those who need more intensive help? Does the teacher use these supports to ensure early literacy success?
- Does the teacher use appropriate technology to promote student interest and excitement in reading?

In addition to these broad questions, you will want to help the teacher analyze instruction in vocabulary development, comprehension and higher-order reading, and connecting writing to reading.

The charts in the resources section can help you and the teacher analyze teacher performance in each area. These areas can also serve as the basis for collaborative goal-setting. Provide the survey to each teacher you work with and encourage them to complete the self-evaluation privately. Ask teachers to write down two or three areas where they want coaching assistance in the next few months.

Together, you will write these into S.M.A.R.T. goals to be mutually worked on during the next few weeks. Putting these into written goals will help you focus everyone's attention on what you are trying to improve and help you better track each teacher's professional development plans. Make sure that your goals are observable and measurable so that you can easily measure and assess progress.

Building Literacy in the High School Classroom

While students still read narrative text in high school English or reading classes, the most common type of text found in high school classrooms is expository text. Since the strategies needed for effective literacy development in the English or reading classroom differ somewhat from the strategies and approaches needed to process expository text in content classrooms, this book will examine those strategies more suited to the content classroom.

Although narrative text strategies will also be provided as may be appropriate, the ideas and strategies contained in *Literacy Strategies for Grades 4-12: Reinforcing the Threads of Reading* (Tankersley, 2005) will provide more specific information that English or reading teachers may find helpful for enhancing literacy instruction in the English or reading classroom.

Expository text includes textbooks, encyclopedias, biographies, topical nonfiction books, scientific documents, and historical or political documents. Expository texts usually provide a reader with information on a specific topic or provide an analysis of an issue. Readers will have differing interest levels, reading proficiency, and background knowledge on the various topics from expository text sources. Generally, readers need to read somewhat carefully and take notes about the information they learn from expository texts to get the most out of them.

Some teachers rely solely on the academic textbook they have been given to present information to students. Vacca and Vacca (2008, p. 8) report, "All too often, academic texts are viewed as sacred canons, authoritative sources of knowledge by which the information in a field is transmitted from generation to generation of learners." Since "one size" never fits all readers in a high school class, a literacy coach can help teachers identify related expository materials that can better meet the reading needs of students.

Functional texts include maps, schedules, diagrams, manuals, and directions. Functional texts provide information to accomplish a specific task, such as using a computer software program, finding a location, preparing a recipe, completing an application, conducting a step-by-step experiment, or constructing something.

Functional texts are used in daily life to accomplish day-to-day tasks. To make the most of information in a functional text, students must understand how to skim for the specific information they need, such as in a manual, or how to read carefully to determine the exact step-by-step procedure and evaluate the details, as in following directions. Content classroom teachers need to identify the various types of expository and functional texts relevant to their content area and think about specific support strategies students may need to read these types of text.

There are many great strategies that teachers can use to prepare students to read, help them process text, and debrief what they have read. This chapter will help you identify the strategies and approaches that will most benefit the teachers with whom you work.

These strategies aim to help students link to what they already know about a topic and connect their new learning to prior knowledge, comprehend more deeply and to greater levels, and remember more of what they read when finished. These strategies can help teachers positively affect student reading achievement, regardless of the student's reading performance level.

In the remainder of this chapter, we will explore strategies to help teachers positively affect student reading achievement. In the resources, you will find a survey on the classroom environment and the various instructional strategies suggested in this Chapter. You can use these instruments to help high school teachers target areas they wish to work on with you during your coaching time. Provide a copy of the survey and ask teachers to privately rank themselves and determine

if there are any areas in which they would like assistance, more information, or more extensive coaching. Then, when you get together, you can focus your time on helping teachers learn the strategies they have selected. When you focus your time on modeling and coaching teachers in these new instructional strategies, they can apply them directly within their daily work with students.

Preparing Students to Read in Content Texts
Establishing Purpose for Reading

Whenever we read something, we consider the type of material, our purpose for reading the specific text, and our motivation for reading it. For example, we may quickly read a magazine article about a favorite movie star. Although our motivation and interest may be high, we will not have to remember this information or do anything further. Therefore, a quick reading of the article will suffice.

Depending on our personal motivation, we may or may not be highly motivated to do the reading thoroughly and well. If we know that we will have to take a test over the content of a chapter and be given a grade on our performance, we will use a slower reading strategy. We will probably even take notes on the material.

Some readers, particularly students who struggle with reading, attempt to use close and careful reading for everything they read. They do not know that good readers understand how to vary their reading style and approach depending on the purpose to be accomplished. Teachers can help students understand these concepts by modeling skimming, scanning, and close reading (with and without note-taking) techniques. They can then guide students in the approaches that might benefit the types of reading they are doing.

Students should always know in advance what they will be expected to do with the knowledge after reading. Will they be expected to take a test, write an essay, complete a graphic organizer, or summarize the key points? Based on the purpose of reading and what they will be expected to do with the information after reading, students can make better decisions about how much detail to use when reading the text.

Activating Background Knowledge

The brain functions most effectively by making connections and linking old knowledge to new knowledge (Sousa, 2005). When teachers help students recall what they already know about a topic, it helps to stimulate thinking and enhance a person's motivation to read the new text.

Some strategies that content teachers can use include brainstorming known facts about the topic, creating KWL or KWWL charts (Ogle, 1986), using an anticipation guide (Heber & Nelson, 1986; Readence, Bean, & Baldwin, 1998), making predictions, or completing various concept maps or graphic organizers as may be appropriate to student's prior learning on the topic."

Some additional strategies teachers might find helpful to establish purpose or help activate background knowledge are described. Many additional strategies for activating prior knowledge can be found in Literacy Strategies for Grades 4-12: Reinforcing the Threads of Reading (Tankersley, 2005). According to Vacca and Vacca (2008), "Two of the most important questions that students can ask about a text are 'What do I need to know?' and 'How well do I already know it?'

Using Prediction

Good readers use prediction when they pick up a book, newspaper, or magazine. From the first moment we look at the title or the headline, we begin making predictions about what content the article or book might contain and our interest level in the topic.

Many students who struggle with reading do not understand how to use prediction skills to guide their reading. They do not understand how to select material that might suit their interests, what they need to find out, or their reading ability. Their idea of "good" reading material is to find the shortest article, the thinnest book, or the one with the biggest print and the largest number of pictures.

One strategy teachers might find helpful is having students look at chapter headings and subheadings in the text they are reading. They can then turn these headings and subheadings into questions that can guide their reading.

For example, a social studies chapter might be called "Working for Equal Rights." It might contain a section heading called "Boycotting Montgomery Buses." Students might write questions such as: Who boycotted the buses? What happened to cause the boycott? When in history did this take place? How was this situation resolved? As students read, they determine which questions have been answered by what they have read in the chapter section. Extra credit can even be awarded for locating the answers in supplemental texts to questions the students have asked, but that have not been answered by the text they have been reading.

Prior Knowledge Jot

This KWL pre-reading activity can help students think about their prior knowledge and understanding. It can help students identify areas of interest. Before beginning the lesson, the teacher either draws on the board or gives a worksheet that is divided into four response areas for the following four questions:

1) "What I know for sure about (topic)";
2) "What I think I know about (topic)";

3) "What I would like to know more about (topic)";
4) "What I have now learned about (topic)."

The teacher instructs students to complete the first three questions before reading the text. This can be done individually, as partners, or in small groups. Students then read the indicated material either silently or as a cooperative group. After reading, students discuss the material and determine any misconceptions they may have had about the topic. They then summarize their learning and respond to the final question, "What I have now learned about (topic)." Teachers can assemble the charts from each group to form a classroom KWL chart to summarize class information.

Predicting Content Information from Keywords

Select eight to ten words from the text that are key to the information contained in the text. Have students examine the words in small groups to determine how the words might fit together. Once students have discussed the words, tell them to place them in a relational graphic organizer to predict how they think the words might fit together.

After reading the text, students compare their predictions to the actual relationships of the words and make any corrections that may be needed to their graphic organizers. Another strategy that can be done with these words is to have students write a prediction paragraph using the provided words logically and connectedly. The paragraph should contain the gist of what students think the text will be about and how the words might fit together in the text.

After students have read the text, they can then return to their predictions to see how accurate they were in predicting how the words might be related to the information provided in the text.

Story or Text Impressions

Story/text impressions (McGinley & Denner, 1987) is a strategy that not only gets students to anticipate the content of a text but also helps them make predictions about the likely content of the text. Select twelve to fifteen words and/or phrases from the text selection. These should be nouns that might be used to write a summary of the text.

For example, if students were to read an article about the events of the United States recession, the teacher might select the following words: "oil prices," "skyrocketing inflation," "gold standard," "airplane fuel," "cost of food," "housing crisis," "cost of gas," "economic confusion," "U.S. economy," "economic prosperity," "value," "prices," "commodity," and "foreign investors."

Students would be asked to think about the relationships between the words and to predict what a summary paragraph containing each of these words might sound like. Using each word, students write a summary of the article as if they had already read it based on their background knowledge and the relationship they believe the words might have in the actual text.

After students have written a coherent summary of what they believe the article will discuss, they share their summaries with the class. Students then read the article to see how close their prediction was to the actual gist of the text. Students can evaluate the contributions and vote for the summary that they feel provides the closest prediction of the content from the article provided. Language Arts teachers can also use story elements such as plot, characters, setting, and so forth to write a summary of a narrative text.

Helping Students Increase Expository Comprehension

At the start of each school year, content area teachers should take time to help students understand the layout and reading assistance features of their course textbooks. They should also help students understand how to be disciplined readers.

Classroom teachers became specialists in their content because they enjoyed their subject area and probably excelled in that specific area as students themselves. As content specialists, they not only have a deep understanding of the concepts involved in "doing" math, science, or social studies, but they also have a good understanding of how to read the text in this discipline.

For example, how is the material organized? Is it chronologically organized or written in a step-by-step, sequential fashion? Is the main idea generally found at the beginning of the paragraph? Is it likely to be found at the end of the paragraph as in a math story problem?

One of the best strategies teachers can use to help their students understand how to process text in their specific content area is reading aloud and modeling how to process the information by thinking aloud.

After teachers help students understand how the content is generally written, they should then help students understand the various support features of the textbook that may be used during the class. Are there questions to guide reading, vocabulary links, inset maps, or charts? Students must be taught how to read and integrate these support materials into actively reading the text.

Kamil (2003, p. 22) reminds us, "…even adolescents and adults have difficulties effectively processing visuals within text." He cautions that teachers must actively teach strategies for comprehending nontextual materials and reminds us, "Many adolescents will need instruction and guided practice with applying strategies for processing nontextual information in meaningful contexts."

Will students benefit by creating graphic organizers (timelines, flow charts, or comparison charts) as they read? Is the text vocabulary dense? How might students connect to new words or identify new uses for vocabulary words they already know?

For example, while students may know the word "table" as a four-legged item with a flat top for holding items, do they understand what a periodic table is? Do they know what to do in math class if asked to construct a matrix table? Are they likely to read a text organized in chronological order or one written with causes and their effects or definitions and examples? Different reading strategies are needed in each case to be successful readers and comprehenders of content knowledge.

Students should also know what reading and comprehension resources have been provided in the text. Are there graphs? An index or glossary? Are there special insets that give examples or more information on the topic? Understanding how a textbook is organized and what reading supports are provided is essential to successful learning.

Once teachers have identified the strategy lessons needed to lay a solid reading foundation beneath student readers, the next step is determining how the reading will be accomplished. Simply telling students to "read the chapter and answer the comprehension questions at the end of the chapter," as many content teachers may have done in the past, will not ensure that students have done more than simply pass their eyes over the text.

Content area teachers need to be introduced to a range of alternative strategies to help students read the intended text and develop a deeper level of comprehension concerning the content of the text. Some strategies are presented below to help teachers ensure students are more motivated to read the assigned material and process the text at deeper levels of understanding.

Group Reading by Section or Topic

One strategy students find interesting and motivational is dividing the chapter into sections or topics. For example, in a science textbook chapter on pollution, the chapter might contain the topics of air pollution, water pollution, soil contamination, noise pollution, and light pollution.

Divide students into groups and assign each group one specific topic to explore in detail. If the text materials need supplementation, additional relevant and appropriate materials on the topic in question may also be provided to the group. Tell each group to read the information on their topic and be prepared to respond to a specific set of questions, such as: What is it? How does it occur? Why is it a problem? What is being done to address the problem of (topic) pollution? Students are given reasonable time to read the provided materials, discuss them, and then formulate a short presentation on their specific topic to the class. As each group presents their information, the audience takes notes on the information and asks the "experts" any questions that they may have on the topic at hand.

Reading Study Guides

Study guides (Alverman, Phelps, & Ridgeway, 2007) can help students determine what is essential to know from a chapter and specify what is to be done with the information in the chapter. One type of reading guide asks students to read at three levels, the literal, the interpretive, and the applied level, to take learning to the deepest level.

For example, at the literal level, the study guide might ask students to identify whether a given set of statements is true or false and ask them to identify the page number where they found the information on this statement.

For the interpretive level, the study guide might ask students to evaluate specific statements to determine whether the reader believes that the author would agree or disagree with specific statements based on what has been presented in the text. Since these statements are not explicitly found in the text, the reader must interpret the information presented and then provide evidence from the text that supports the response.

At the applied level, the teacher might ask students to use the information learned in the text to write whether they agree or disagree with a specific statement regarding the topic and provide supportive evidence from the text. Not only does this require students to synthesize and apply what they have read from the text, but it also helps students understand how to respond to similar items frequently appearing on the constructed response sections of many state tests.

Sticky Note Reading

Ask students to read a specific section of text with a partner. Provide each group two small pads of "sticky notes" in two colors. As they read, students are directed to mark questions they had while reading or places where they had an idea or made a connection with something they already knew. Students may read the section either silently or aloud to one another, stopping at the end of each section in the text to discuss what they have read.

As they read, students identify two or three questions they had about the text, marking the section with a specific color sticky note. On each sticky note, they record their question and place it in the text at the appropriate point in the passage. The second color sticky note marks places where the pair connected to something they already knew, had an idea, read about the concept in a different text, or heard the teacher say something about the topic. Again, students jot down their connection on the sticky note and place it in the text at the appropriate place. After each group has completed the reading task and has placed their sticky notes in the text, the teacher leads a discussion of questions and connections regarding the reading with the class.

Stopping Points

The teacher assigns a specific amount of text, such as a small section or a page or two, and provides a specific "stopping point" in the text. Everyone reads to the stopping point as directed. When everyone has finished the text section, the teacher asks students to orally summarize the information. The summary is orally conducted, and questions or misunderstandings are addressed as needed. When the section is adequately summarized and clarified, the teacher assigns the next section to be read, and the process is repeated.

Alternating Partners Read and Discuss

Before beginning the reading assignment, the teacher prepares a handout of assignments for student partners A and B. For example, the teacher may provide the first direction: "Together, both partners look at the headlines and subtopics in this reading section. Then person A reads paragraph 1 on page 300 aloud. Once this has been completed, briefly discuss with your partner what you predict this section will be about. Write down with your partner at least four predictions of what you think you will learn in this section in the space on your handout." The next direction might then be provided for person B or may suggest that the partners do something together. The teacher details how each section will be read (skim, scan, or do a close reading of the section with notes) and tells students what to discuss or record on their handout about that section of the text. After partners have had time to read the text and complete the requested discussions or written activities, the teacher debriefs with a classroom discussion on the sections of the text read.

Listening to Text

For classrooms with many struggling readers, an excellent strategy is to record or ask a volunteer to orally read and record the text segment on a tape or CD. When students are reading silently, the struggling readers can listen to the exact text being read aloud while following along in the text. To develop the comprehension skills of the listener even further, at key points in the text, the reader can even stop and summarize what has been read so that the listener gets used to hearing the material synthesized as the reading continues.

Content Comprehension Fix-Up

Teachers work with other teachers who teach the same content area to identify the fix-up strategies best used with this content area. For example, some helpful strategies might include: slowing the reading pace, reading aloud, looking back and re-read the sentence or the paragraph, looking ahead for clues that might provide more information, using a glossary or dictionary for unknown terms, restating an idea, or ask someone else for clarification or help. Teachers specifically teach students how to use appropriate fix-up strategies, model these aloud for students and then place them on a classroom chart as a reminder of the appropriate strategies that might help clarify meaning.

Clarifying and Demonstrating Understanding

The purpose of reading is to help students gain meaning and learn new information regarding a content area. As a result, after reading, content area teachers want to know that students have learned the material, have thought about the information, and have made connections between this new information and the background knowledge they already possess. The more ways that new learning is grounded and connected to prior learning, the stronger the retention and understanding of the material. The National Reading Panel Report (2000) identifies seven categories of comprehension instruction that meet the panel's rigorous criteria for effective practice following reading. These 7 strategies include comprehension monitoring, cooperative learning, use of graphic and semantic organizers, answering questions generated from the text, generating questions based on the text, examining story or text structure, and summarizing what was read. In addition to these essential strategies, some excellent additional strategies you can help teachers implement after reading include the following techniques. For more extensive after-reading strategies, see *Literacy Strategies for Grades 4-12: Reinforcing the Threads of Reading* (Tankersley, 2005).

My Translation Paragraphs

Good readers often read complex paragraphs several times and think about the meaning of what they are reading to ensure good comprehension. When struggling readers read text, they often give up if the meaning is not immediately apparent. One strategy that can help students get used to re-reading and thinking about the meaning of their reading is by creating "translations" for the paragraphs in the text students have read. Divide a text passage into segments and assign partners or trios one segment each to read. Once students have read the passage, they should rewrite it or "translate" it into everyday language. Once all groups have completed their translations, have each group read their plain English translation to the class in the order in which it occurs in the passage. Not only does this strategy help students discuss and ensure they understand what is being said, but by putting it into their own words, they have placed it deeper into cognitive memory.

Knowledge Web

Students read a specific section of text either individually or with partners. When they have completed the task, students work with a group of three or four to create a "knowledge web" of the ideas presented in the text on sheets of chart paper. At first, students create their web from memory; however, after creating a preliminary web, they can review the text to add to the web, fix inaccurate information, or clarify specific information to add more detail to the web. After each group has created their knowledge web, charts are presented to the class and reviewed for accuracy. If time permits, illustrations can also be added to the knowledge web to add interest and help cement learning.

Drawing the Text

Since students benefit from having more senses involved in the reading process, an excellent strategy for clarifying what has been read is to have students create a visual of some type to represent the information they have read. To begin, place students in groups of three or four and give each group a sheet of butcher paper and a set of markers. Ask students to visually represent what they have read in the text. When the groups have completed their visuals, have them present and explain their drawings and their connections.

Talk Through

A valuable strategy developed by Simpson (1995) is the "talk through" strategy, which helps readers share their thinking about a text. Assign a specific text section and allow students time to read the material silently. Allow students a brief amount of time to discuss what they have read with a small group of three or four. After students have had a few minutes to review the material with their group, ask various students or groups to "talk through" specific components in the text. For example, a science teacher might tell students, "Talk through how this process takes place." A math teacher might say, "Talk through what we must do to perform this algorithm." An English teacher might say, "Talk through the connections your group made as you read this story." Engaging students at this level of cognitive processing forces them to think more deeply about the text and to process it at high levels.

Thinking Aloud

One of the frustrations of content teachers across the country is that students sometimes do not fare well on constructed response sections of the state content test for their subject area. One way to help students become more comfortable with the type of deep thinking required on state assessments is by using the "thinking aloud" strategy. Assign a section of text to be read, and then ask students to perform an activity similar to one they might be presented with on a state content assessment. For example, if students are expected to use a map to draw conclusions and make recommendations on the state assessment, be sure that this is the same task they are asked to do following the reading.

After students have had time to write a response on paper to the requested activity, have them "think aloud" to the class about what they wrote and what thinking they used to process the response. This task benefits math and science, where students must process complex tasks and arrive at logical conclusions. Hearing other students' thinking aloud is helpful to all learners, particularly those who struggle with reading comprehension.

Quick Writes

"Quick writes" are an easy way to determine what students know and understand due to their learning. Quick writes can be used to assess what has been learned or to help students self-assess their own understandings. To help students synthesize what was learned, ask students to take out a piece of paper and to write for three to five minutes on a specific topic, such as "Define 'equilateral' in your own words" or "Write in words what this formula means" or "What causes an airplane to fly?" and similar types of questions. To analyze what students do not understand or still are confused

172

about, you can have them write responses to questions like: "What did you not understand about today's lesson?" or "List one or more terms that you cannot clearly define and describe what is still confusing for you." or "What could I change about today's lesson to help you better understand the concepts and ideas?" A quick glance over student work can inform you about what students still need to have clarified or whether or not they have truly understood the concepts presented in the lesson.

Differentiating for Diverse Learner Needs

Content teachers face an increasingly diverse group of learners who present unique learning challenges nationwide. While this book presents reading strategies that can benefit all types of readers and learners, some specific suggestions for working with non-English-speaking students might also be helpful to literacy coaches working with classroom teachers.

Helpful strategies for content area teachers are using strategies that help students say, write, and visually represent concepts so that students are presented with learning clarification in many ways. Another successful strategy is providing reading tasks in smaller chunks and allowing plenty of time for students to talk with one another about the material.

Comprehension significantly rises when students can orally process and use partner or small group discussions about the material. Strategies that help students activate their prior knowledge and process information with greater clarity, including those discussed in this chapter, are also beneficial for diverse learners in the classroom.

Building and Reinforcing Vocabulary

There is a strong correlation between vocabulary knowledge and reading comprehension (Vacca & Vacca, 2008). In synthesizing the recent research on vocabulary development, Baker, Simmons & Kameenui (1995) found that extensive vocabulary size differences between students occur early in a child's life. This gap grows increasingly significant over time.

Bog and Anders (1990) found that students who worked in groups and performed semantic mapping or semantic feature analysis outperformed students who learned new vocabulary by definition only.

Baumann & Kameenui (1991) report success with the "keyword" method. In this method, students draw a picture based on the word's sound that also links to the word's meaning. For example, to remember the definition of the word "catacomb," a student might draw a cat (based on the word's sound) in a winding, underground tunnel with recesses for graves in the walls. The picture can help students easily remember that the word catacomb represents an "underground chamber for graves or a winding underground tunnel."

Students need to encounter words multiple times before they become a permanent part of the student's usable vocabulary set. In addition to direct word instruction, another valuable technique is using affixes to break down new words into their prefixes, suffixes, and root words.

This technique and context information can help students unlock the meaning of many new content words and word families. See Chapter 3 of *Literacy: Strategies for Grades 4-12: Reinforcing the Threads of Reading* (Tankersley, 2005) for additional information regarding the importance of vocabulary to strong reading achievement and many additional strategies content area teachers may find helpful for vocabulary instruction.

As a reading coach, you can help content teachers consider the keywords with which students must be familiar to read relevant text materials. At the start of the year, it would be helpful to have teams of content teachers get together to identify the key vocabulary words that students need to know to be successful with the content subject matter by unit.

Have teachers then identify which words can be learned by separating the word into component parts and studying the prefix, suffix, and roots of the word; which words might lend themselves to visual interpretations; and which words might best be taught using semantic feature webs, concept maps, or pictorial vocabulary maps, such as Frayer charts (Frayer, Frederick, & Klausmeier, 1969), to provide students with characteristics and examples and non-examples of the keyword. Content vocabulary journals or logs can also be helpful additions to the content classroom so students can continue building vocabulary fluency.

At the start of the school year, encourage teachers to devote space to developing a "word wall" where new words can be placed so that students continue to see the words throughout the school year. When teachers analyze their vocabulary words and determine the best strategies to teach each word, students will have a greater chance of learning and retaining the word for the long term.

Technology

A recent study (Lenhart et al., 2008) found that 47 percent of adolescent bloggers write for personal reasons several times a week outside of school, with one-quarter of these individuals writing on a daily basis. Only 33 percent of nonblogging adolescents wrote outside of school.

The study also reported that 65 percent of adolescent bloggers perceived writing as essential to their later success. In comparison, only 53 percent of nonblogging teens held this belief. Students indicated that what motivated them to engage in self-initiated writing was being responsible to their audiences by creating engaging and informative writing. A whopping 78 percent of all adolescent respondents reported that teachers should employ more use of digital writing tools to motivate students to do more writing.

When researching information online, students often turn to major search engines, such as Google, Yahoo Search, or Ask, to locate resources and information. This may lead students to nonscholarly information or to waste time sifting through irrelevant sites.

Teachers can help students locate more appropriate scholarly materials by accessing library sites such as InfoTrac Junior Edition, Academic Search Premier, Galeschools, CQ Researcher, or General Reference Center Gold. Check with your media center specialist regarding which databases are available in your school for students conducting research.

Be sure to model for students how to search and evaluate the relevance and reliability of any information they find. You can introduce students to the Web monitoring sites, such as https://snopes.com, which help identify problematic sites on the Internet.

You can also introduce students to digital notetaking. Tools such as PC NoteTaker, Google NoteBook, FreeMind, KeyNote, or Web Notes let students organize their notes and place them into their writing drafts. Teachers should model the process of synthesizing the information they read into notes for students. Students can often subscribe to email newsletters, podcasts or receive text messages about their topics of interest.

Another excellent tool for students to use in organizing what they will be writing about is mind-mapping software. Some school districts have software such as Inspiration or Kidspiration. You can also use free sites if your district does not have this software. Some examples include https://bubbl.us, Lucidspark, Miro, or Ayoa, just a few of the many mind-mapping tools available on the Internet.

While many schools continue to fight against cell phone presence in high schools nationwide, others know how to use cell phones to benefit learning. For example, students can use their cell phones to create short videos about a topic for others to view. They can scan QR codes to connect with videos or relevant texts on a unit of study. While working on writing assignments, students can access online resources such as dictionaries and other necessary reference books.

Teachers and students can create and use polling software, such as https://www.polleverywhere.com, where teachers can ask students to express their opinions via voting through texting. These are just a few ways teachers are incorporating technology into student learning.

The International Society for Technology in Education (ISTE) has a helpful video of a classroom teacher explaining how her teaching has changed since incorporating technology into the classroom that teachers might find helpful. You can find her video on YouTube at https://youtu.be/hJ37VZ82aNY (2020). Teachers love it, as do students, since they use technology they are familiar with and use in their daily lives.

Conclusion

In addition to examining best practices in reading, the National Reading Panel (2000) also examined the connection between teacher professional development and reading achievement. They concluded that teachers did learn new concepts and could implement these into their instructional programs. Pang & Kamil (2003) further examined studies that reported both teacher and student data about student reading achievement. They stated, "Most important, if there were no gains for teachers, there were no gains for students. Thus, if teachers did not learn what was taught, students did not experience gains in reading performance." (p. 25).

When high school reading coaches can help teachers identify key strategies that can support their discipline and lead to greater comprehension of the material to be learned, student achievement improves, and stronger readers are built.

In conclusion, this chapter has equipped literacy coaches working with middle and high school teachers with invaluable information and effective reading strategies explicitly tailored for grades 6-12. By embracing the ideas presented within this chapter, literacy coaches can not only fulfill the needs of teachers but also cultivate impactful job-embedded support that ultimately enhances student achievement. With these insights, literacy coaches can play a pivotal role in shaping a more successful future for teachers and their students.

"As soon as the word improvement enters the teaching conver-sation, we tend to get defensive because to suggest we need to improve implies that what we are doing right now is not good enough. Yet we know that what we are currently doing isn't meeting every child's needs, and even though we proclaim that we believe "all children can learn," we know that we are fail-ing large groups of students. While acknowledging that our students' literacy skills are lacking, we feel unprepared to teach literacy, especially if we presumed our upper elementary, middle, and high school students would come to us already reading and writing well."
(Casey, 2006, p. 23)

Chapter 4

Planning for Coaching

To help the adults with whom we work to grow and improve their instructional skills, we first must understand how adult learning takes place. Adults must be responsible for their learning and en-couraged to self-reflect on their skills and practices.

As the building coach, your role is to get teachers' perspectives about what they want to learn and help them work on projects that meet their interests and perceived needs. To grow, they need to be open to learning how a new practice might impact their perfor-mance and be free to direct their own work. It would be best if you acted as a facilitator, guiding those with whom you work to think about their practices and identify new strategies and approaches to help them reach their goals.

The most effective professional growth occurs when teachers take ownership of what they want to learn and can connect to how it will make a difference for their students. Teachers must understand and connect with the reason for learning a new skill. They must find the learning relevant to what they do on a daily basis and help them see how the new ideas or strategies might be helpful to them in their work.

We must also respect adults as people who can bring a wealth of experiences to our instructional team. We must value their experience and knowledge and allow them to voice their opinions and ideas even when we know they may not have the "whole picture" at that point. As we do for children, we must scaffold adult learners from where they are to where they need and want to go—moving forward one step at a time as they are ready to climb to higher proficiency levels.

Coaches can help teachers expand their thinking and set purposeful goals for student learning and their own learning. They can also help each teacher identify strategies and techniques that are relevant and practical to add to their instructional repertoire.

Some roles that you may play in your building as the instructional or reading coach are:

- •To work collaboratively with building administration and classroom teachers to enhance instruction and student learning in reading across the curriculum.
- •To collaborate with individual teachers and encourage teacher teams to identify the key skills that students need to demonstrate at that grade level, plan focused and targeted standards-based instruction, provide modeling and support

when introducing new concepts or strategies that will strengthen learning, suggest solutions to barriers or problems, team teach with grade-level teachers to provide support and modeling, and provide informal observational coaching as may be requested by individual teachers.

•To support the professional growth of teachers by helping them reflect on their own practices and the results that they are getting with their students, identify assessments (both formal and informal) that will tell teachers if students have learned what they intended to teach, and, finally, help teachers learn and apply more effective teaching practices that result in more effective student learning.

•To lead professional study groups and conduct interest-based professional development sessions specific to the needs of grade-level teams or groups of teachers.

•Assist teachers and administrators in interpreting assessment results and student achievement strengths and weaknesses.

•To assist in developing effective instructional strategies, classroom assessments, end-of-course assessments, and how to evaluate the quality of student work samples in various content areas.

•Assist teachers in creating formal and informal assessments that measure skills and concepts teachers have taught.

•Assist teachers in locating and adapting resources appropriate for each content area and the diverse needs of students.

•Support and act as a sounding board for veteran and first-year teachers as needed to encourage, focus, and enable success.

We now have a deeper understanding of what helps students develop solid reading skills; however, remember the old saying about being able to lead the horse to water but not being able to make him drink. That is true for teachers with whom you work as well. You can help them reflect on their practices. However, growth only occurs when the teacher chooses their own path for growth and sees the connections between the changes they are attempting to make and increased student success.

Since self-improvement must begin with a thoughtful self-analysis of current knowledge, understandings, and practice, the resources section checklists can help teachers reflect on their practices and instructional skills. As Fullen (2007) reminds us, "Educational change depends on what teachers do and think—it's as simple and as complex as that."

The role of the literacy coach is to help classroom teachers identify the types of texts students will need to process in each content area and then help teachers understand effective strategies to support reading development with each type of text.

As Kamil states (2003, p. 29) in his report *Adolescents and Literacy: Reading for the 21ˢᵗ Century*:

> But there is a strong body of research-based knowledge that is available about adolescent literacy. This research demonstrates that we do know enough about adolescent literacy to make positive changes today. We know a great deal about the literacy needs of adolescents and about the teaching practices that are effective for them. We know that skills such as decoding and fluency lead to better reading comprehension. We know that motivation and encouragement are critical elements for adolescents. We know that English-language learners face additional challenges when learning to read and write

well in English. And we know that professional development for teachers has positive effects on student reading achievement.

Working with Teachers to Establish Instructional Focus

All lessons must begin with a focused instructional goal in mind. From our instruction, we need to be able to quickly assess who gets it and is ready to move on and who still needs more support or practice to be able to do what we want them to do. In other words, after instruction, ask teachers, "What can students do now that they couldn't do before the instruction took place?"

If teachers have no clear idea about what they expect their students to do differently after instruction, the lesson lacks focus. As Stiggins and colleagues (Stiggins et al., 2004) are quick to remind us, if we don't begin with the end in mind, we won't know if our students are making progress.

Here is an example of what I mean by this statement. When I dropped into the classroom a week before Valentine's Day, a first-grade teacher was having her students draw and color pictures in a paper booklet that she had cut and stapled into a small booklet with about twelve pages. On each page, she had written the words in bold letters "Love is…". Her instructions to her students were to draw a picture of something showing the meaning of love on each page of the booklet as a Valentine's Day gift for their parents. It was 9:00 in the morning, and her schedule on the whiteboard stated that this was her ELA instructional block.

Although most of her first-graders were reading and writing at grade level by this point in the school year, the only activity was picture drawing. The children were dutifully spending a substantial amount of class time creating lovely pictures showing what they perceived as acts of love on the 12 pages of their little books. Students were not asked to use their writing skills to explain the pictures they were laboriously drawing on each page.

Later in the day, I met with her about her lesson. I asked her what her students had learned or could do as a result of this lesson that moved their learning forward in some way. She became defensive and told me it was an "art" lesson and students were creating a special "gift" for their mothers for Valentine's Day. She also wanted her students to have some fun on Valentine's Day.

While I certainly want students to enjoy school and their learning, the lesson could have been fun and practical for students. Students could have practiced their writing skills on an authentic and meaningful task had she asked more of them. How much time is wasted in classrooms across America on activities or tasks that do not move students forward in their learning objectives?

We all know that time is of the essence in schools nowadays. There is no time to waste on "fluff" or lessons that do not have a solid link to the grade-level standards. While the teacher's favorite lesson on butterflies or the chateaus of France might be fun and engaging unless it is explicitly built on the skills and understandings prescribed in the state and district standards.

Instructional time is already short in the school day. There is no point wasting time on lessons that do not align with grade-level expectations nor result in improved student learning. As coaches, we can help teachers understand that all instruction must be tied with laser-like focus to the skills we need students to learn and the proficiency targets students must meet.

According to Schmoker & Marzano (1999), in districts making significant student achievement gains,

> Teachers knew exactly what students needed to learn, what to teach to, where to improve, and what to work on with colleagues." They state, "Make no mistake: The success of any organization is contingent upon clear, commonly defined goals. A well-articulated focus unleashes individual and collective energy. And a common focus clarifies understanding, accelerates communication, and promotes persistence and collective purpose (Rosenholtz, 1991). This is the stuff of improvement.

Stiggins et al. (2004) distinguishes between assessment *for* learning and assessment *of* learning. They say, "Assessments of learning are those assessments that happen after learning is supposed to have occurred to determine if it did," while "assessments for learning happen while learning is still underway.

We conduct these types of assessments throughout teaching and learning. They help us diagnose student needs and plan our next steps in instruction. They also provide students with feedback they can use to improve the quality of their work and feel in control of their journey to success.

These researchers point out (p.39) that teachers can increase student motivation to learn when students:

1) have a sense of control and choice;
2) get frequent and specific feedback on their performance;
3) encounter tasks that are challenging but not overwhelming;
4) can accurately self-assess their own performance;
5) encounter learning tasks related to everyday life.

By helping teachers reflect on how they assess student mastery of the learning objectives during instruction and providing the correct motivational context for learning to occur, we are helping teachers become more effective practitioners.

Teachers must be able to identify what students should be able to do as a result of instruction. They should also know how they will determine if students can demonstrate their knowledge or skills. When teachers clearly understand these two elements, designing the correct instructional sequence and providing the correct modeling and support students need to produce the desired results is much easier. This is strategic teaching.

Classroom teachers can learn much about strategic teaching from teachers who work in performance-centered content areas such as music, art, or physical education. For example, if the basketball coach wanted students to be able to make a basket every time they approached the free-throw line, the coach would model the proper technique at the free-throw line, demonstrating how to put the ball through the hoop from this location while students watched (modeling).

He would then ask students to practice many shots by standing at the free-throw line and attempting to put the ball through the hoop (independent practice). Students would continue to practice the skill until most of the group could execute the action with some skill.

While students were practicing, the coach would watch and give specific, corrective feedback to individuals who needed help to achieve mastery (corrective feedback). The coach might also give a couple of students who were particularly advanced an additional tip or specialized movement (enrichment) and may ask a couple of students to come in for additional help with the needed skill after school (remediation.)

In *Classroom Assessment for Student Learning: Doing it Right, Using it Well* (Stiggins et al., 2004), the authors cite seven critical practices observed in the most effective classrooms:

1) a clear and understandable vision of the learning target that students are expected to achieve;

2) examples and models of both strong and weak work;

3) frequent and descriptive feedback to students;

4) teaching students to self-assess and to set their own learning goals;

5) designing lessons that focus on one aspect of quality at a time;

6) teaching students to make focused revisions of their work; and, finally,

7) encouraging students to self-reflect, keep track of their learning progress, and share their learning with the teacher and others.

When providing feedback to students about their learning, teachers sometimes overlook the importance of clearly addressing learning performance. It is crucial to go beyond mere feedback and ensure that students understand their current performance and what they need to do to improve. Like a basketball coach, who knows that players' refinement and improvement occur when they engage in self-reflection and take action based on feedback, students also enhance their performance by reflecting on the feedback provided by their teachers and making necessary adjustments.

To support teachers in identifying areas where students may require additional assistance, literacy coaches can serve as an additional set of eyes. They collaborate with teachers, helping them determine how to proceed with feedback, explicit practice, and support. By fostering a culture of self-reflection and self-evaluation among teachers, we can empower them to become lifelong learners themselves, which ultimately leads to higher success for their students.

Scaffolding Teacher Learning

To help teachers improve their reading instruction, coaches should help them focus on one or two key strategies or ways to improve their classroom performance at a time. By keeping it simple, teachers can move from novice to proficient in a much shorter period. To help a new instructional practice become a comfortable and frequently used part of a teacher's instructional "bags of tricks," the teacher needs to weave the strategies into their regular classroom routine until they are familiar with and can easily use the new practice with their students regularly.

For example, if a fourth-grade teacher wanted to learn to use echo reading, choral reading, repeated readings, and readers' theater to help their students become more fluent and expressive readers, the coach might start by demonstrating echo and choral reading for the teacher in their classroom.

Once the teacher watches and takes notes on how these techniques are modeled with their own students, the coach will move on to the next step. They might provide the teacher with appropriate passages that align with the teacher's content standards. The instructional coach might then discuss (or even model) what using new techniques with students might look like.

As the teacher designs and presents their own lesson, the coach observes the teacher using the new techniques and takes notes. The coach debriefs the teacher by asking them to self-analyze what was successful and where improvement might improve student success. This self-reflection strengthens the teacher's ability to reflect on and identify their performance in the future.

Once the teacher is comfortable implementing echo and choral reading without assistance, the coach might model a new reading skill with which the teacher is unfamiliar. For example, the coach might model how to have students learn to improve fluency and polish their reading by reading and rereading a Readers' Theater text in classroom groups. The coach would place students in collaborative groups and model for students how to practice reading and re-reading the text with appropriate pacing and strong reading expression.

The teacher would implement the technique until they were confident and comfortable using it to improve student reading fluency. After the teacher can successfully implement the technique, the coach can ask the teacher to self-assess and self-reflect on how to improve their performance without the coach's assistance.

As the teacher grows in skill, the coach helps them move toward independence and self-analysis as much as possible. Teacher and coach continue on a cycle of repeatedly experimenting with a new instructional technique, reassessing, and refining, and then beginning the cycle again to expand the teacher's performance and student success.

"A teacher cannot provide assistance in the zone of proximal development (ZPD) unless she knows where the learner is in the developmental process (p. 198). Coaches must make careful observations of the teachers with whom they will be working as well. Coaches and teachers learn from one another just as students and teachers learn from one another."
Gallimore, R., & R. Tharp (1990)

Chapter 5

Building Teacher Capacity
and Independence

To build independence and capacity in our teachers, we must help them make solid connections between what they are currently doing in the classroom and more effective ways to organize and present their subject matter to students. As with students, we must identify current performance levels, determine the next steps, and scaffold teacher learning. This will ensure they have a bridge to help them increase their knowledge and skills. Teachers must be able to connect in their own minds about how the new way of thinking or strategy you want them to blend into their teaching will impact their students or help them become better teachers.

Early in my career, I learned to identify a teacher's level of expertise before trying to assist them in their personal growth. My school had been working on improving math instruction that year. As our teachers listened to an outstanding presenter talk about hands-on math strategies, my mind was racing with how I could help teachers implement some of these new ideas and strategies.

The mood in the room was upbeat, and teachers were clearly connecting to the ideas and strategies being discussed.

To my left sat a thirty-year veteran math teacher who taught in a very traditional, pencil-and-paper manner. His methodologies were so old-fashioned that even my parents would have felt comfortable learning math in his classroom.

Until then, I had made little progress with changing his teaching philosophy or improving his practice in any meaningful way. He felt his classroom worked well and that his students performed well enough.

While his classroom was well managed and student scores were reasonably good on state tests, student motivation, and interest often waned in his class. He often blamed complained about the "kids of today" and their lack of interest in his class. He blamed their disinterest and lack of engagement on his students and demographic changes in the community rather than his methodologies.

While students learned to do the algorithms he taught them by substituting numbers into the formulas he had them memorize, they often lacked a deep understanding of the concepts underlying their learning. As a result, I felt his instruction could have benefited from more up-to-date, hands-on strategies that might engage his students more.

As the teacher listened to our presenter, I noticed that he took copious notes and seemed to be engaged in the presentation. I was hopeful that he might find something beneficial to use in his teaching. During a break, I leaned over and queried, "Well, what do you think, Dan?" He nodded and then described his idea for incorporating something the presenter had just been discussing into his math class.

As he talked, my mind was racing three steps ahead with other ideas he could also do with his students. When he finished telling me his idea, I blurted out, "Yeah, that's a great idea, and then you could do…and…." As I talked, I could see a confused look on his face. He frowned, waved his hand in a patting motion, and said, "Now, simmer down. I'm not *that* excited." I stopped mid-sentence, and we both had a good laugh. I smiled and said, "OK. I get it. Let's try your idea and see how it works." After all, forward motion was still forward motion.

This experience was a valuable lesson that I tried to remember when working with veteran teachers that I wanted to mentor. No matter how much sense the ideas made to me, Dan simply was not ready for anything more advanced than the idea he had just verbalized. As the quote at the start of this chapter says, an effective coach must understand where the teacher is in their thinking and their developmental processes before we can offer support.

Armed with an understanding of the teacher's mindset and willingness to accept support and new ideas, we can scaffold appropriate experiences that help move each teacher forward from their proximal development zone. Dan did incorporate a few new ideas into his teaching, but it was at his own pace and time frame. I realized that I needed to let Dan crawl before I tried to push him to walk or run. Although he retired two years later, he did make some changes that led to higher student motivation. Forward progress is still forward progress.

If we want to be effective coaches, we must first understand a bit about human psychology. According to Glasser (1998), everyone has five basic human needs: survival, love and belonging, power, freedom, and fun. Professor Richard Sagor, in his book *Motivating Students and Teachers in an Era of Standards* (2003), summarized the motivational interests of classroom teachers as follows: competence, belonging, usefulness, potency, and optimism. Sagor says that a person's basic need to feel competent is fulfilled when they receive positive work feedback.

Teachers must, therefore, be given "regular opportunities to validate the positive effects that their work is having on their students' lives." Sagor says that in this era of high accountability, isolationism leads to an unhealthy degree of stress, depression, and, ultimately, teacher burnout.

Collegial and collaborative relationships that help teachers solve the problems they face in their classrooms help teachers have a sense of belonging. This, in turn, enables them to take pride in their accomplishments and efforts. When teachers feel they can make a difference in their student's lives, their sense of usefulness increases. Success breeds more success, and self-confidence increases.

What Glasser calls a need for "power" in our lives, Sagor calls a need for "potency." Sagor says, "When people have valid reasons to believe that they have influence over the factors that affect their ultimate success, they are more likely to exercise that influence." Conversely, if we doubt our capacity to effect the changes necessary to improve our situation, it is understandable we see little point in trying to affect change.

Sagor says that teachers also need to be optimistic in their work. He says,

> With repeated experiences that provide teachers with credible evidence that they are good (competent), that they are part of a quality team (belong), that they have the capacity to make a critical difference in students' lives (useful), and that they have the power (potency) to overcome whatever comes up, then the uncertainties of the future will become far less fearsome.

When we help teachers meet their basic needs, we can create that sense of competency and optimism vital for teacher success.

Building a Coaching Relationship

Establishing a supportive relationship with your teaching staff is essential in every coaching relationship. Teachers and coaches need to have mutual respect and trust for one another. Teachers must see you as a helpful and supportive peer, not a direct line to the administrative staff. It takes time to develop a solid coaching relationship, and there are various phases that this partnership will go through.

The first phase is the "getting started" or "getting to know you" phase. During this phase, the coach and teacher develop a respectful personal relationship. During this time, you will get to know the teacher more personally. Who are they as a person? What is their background, home life, and personal story? What are their interests, goals, hopes, and dreams?

During this time, the coach listens and learns about the teacher and their needs and skills. This will help you deepen trust and learn what to expect and not expect from one another. If the teacher is a willing participant in the coaching process, this time will likely pass very quickly.

If coaching has been chosen *for* the teacher, the coach, and the teacher will likely need more time learning about each other, developing trust, and establishing roles and relationships. During the getting started phase, it can be helpful for the coach to administer a survey to learn more about the teacher, their hopes for coaching, and their needs.

Once the coach and teacher have established a positive rapport and a working relationship, the next phase is the "making progress" phase. Thinking back to what we learned about Bridges' transitions, when the teacher becomes open to learning from the coach, they move into the change process. They will be new skills and letting go of old ways. They may be feeling excited. However, they may also occasionally feel overwhelmed and exhausted, depending on the magnitude of the changes they are expected to make.

Teachers are open to taking chances and trying new behaviors during this time. The coach can help the teacher set "bite-sized" goals and performance targets. These can be called "Goldilocks goals" because they should be "just right goals" – not too small or too large.

Coaches can help their teachers stay on track, maintain the pace, and continue the momentum. Because the stage can be exhausting if teachers take on a significant innovation, some may want to slow down or take a break from coaching. This is normal. However, it should be discouraged since backward slides can happen without continued coaching. This is a vital time for coaches to encourage, support, and point out successes.

The last phase of the coaching relationship is the "renewal phase." During this phase, teachers have experienced success and have developed new ways of thinking. Several goals may have been reached and should be celebrated.

The two co-workers have high trust when the coach-teacher relationship has been solidly formed. New goals can now emerge that will help the teacher's instruction improve even more. The teacher feels confident, is open to new ideas, and is more willing to take risks. During this phase, the coach can help the teacher reflect on their strengths and challenges. Together the partners can determine the best path to continue building on the teacher's successes.

The motivational factors we discussed at the beginning of this chapter help people move toward the desired results. The more you learn about what motivates your teachers, the better your chance of creating a successful partnership.

The coach assists the teacher in staying on track with their goals. They gently hold the teacher accountable for what they said they would do, always remembering that the coach is a supporter, not an evaluator.

Teachers want to make a difference in the lives of their students. When a teacher's performance does not match the expectation of the organization, factors such as a lack of meaningful feedback, unclear expectations, fear of failure, a mismatch between the employee and position, a lack of experience, unclear payoff, or limiting beliefs might be to blame (Reiss, 2007).

Through active listening and powerful questioning, the coach can help the teacher uncover the motivation to make a change or identify the resistance behind not doing what they have been asked to do. Motivation is much higher when the teacher is clear about their purpose, educational beliefs and values, and the job they are expected to do.

Resisting Change

So, why do teachers resist change? The vast number of books on change and resistance in humans line the library shelves. However, there are some fundamental reasons why teachers tend to resist making changes to their instructional practice.

The most straightforward reason teachers resist change is that they already feel the approaches they use are the right ones. Like my math teacher, Dan, they feel competent and comfortable with their current methodology and do not see a need to change what they do. If teachers didn't wholeheartedly believe that what they were doing was the right thing to do, they would actively seek change on their own.

Fullan & Stiegelbauer (1991) identified several factors that can cause teachers to resist change in their practice when new innovations are introduced in a school. They say teachers will resist a new initiative when they do not understand how it will improve learning or make a difference for their students.

Resistance can also occur when there is poor communication about the innovation and how teachers will benefit from learning the new process, routine, or strategy. Changing from comfortable strategies and routines is often perceived as a threat to competence. Humans naturally fear failure, especially when it comes to their careers and their welfare.

Making a difference is the fundamental reason that most teachers became teachers. Their fears, real or not, make them afraid they might no longer make a difference with their students. As a result, they resist adopting the new innovation and continue to stick with what is comfortable and "safe." For experienced teachers like Dan, their present situation seems to work quite well. Therefore, in their minds, they see little incentive to change what is already working well enough. If they change their practice, those changes might be less effective.

We all resist change for the same reasons, so understanding the thinking behind resistance is critical to helping teachers grow and improve. As Michael Jordan says, "Obstacles don't have to stop you. If you run into a wall, don't turn around and give up. Figure out how to climb it, go through it, or work around it." (www.brainyquote.com). If you encounter resistive teachers, continue trying to help each one make a connection with how a new practice will help them be more effective and productive with their students. To be successful, help them take the small steps they are willing to take toward implementing the new innovation.

Because of this natural resistance to change, coaches need to help teachers see how the practices they are trying to instill will improve teaching effectiveness. Build trust and help teachers see that they make a difference in the lives of their students.

As your teachers become more self-confident and comfortable, your relationship will also become stronger and more meaningful for both of you. Understand that by letting go of an old way of doing something, there can be feelings of loss and even grief for some individuals.

The Stages of Change

According to William Bridges (1991) in his well-known book *Managing Transitions*, there are three zones that people pass through during change. The first is the "ending phase," the second is the "neutral phase," and finally, people enter into the "new beginnings" phase.

In the ending phase, some people may experience these emotions as anger, sadness, anxiety, confusion, or even depression.

There may be feelings of losing something important or being forced to relinquish something they are comfortable with or value. Bridges calls this stage the "bridge between the old and the new" way of doing things.

As their partner in the change process, you can help them by nonjudgmentally accepting their feelings. Listen empathetically and communicate openly and positively. Help them understand how they can take the best parts of what they have done in the past and combine it with their new learning.

The neutral phase is the "in-between" place when the individual is not "there" anymore. The neutral phase can be confusing and frustrating as the individual tries to discard the old and accept the new. They may exhibit low morale, anxiety, or skepticism that the change will not improve performance. Still, they have not yet completely transitioned to the "new" way of doing things.

Some people have difficulty moving through the neutral phase without support and reassurance that they are progressing. As a coach, help your teachers acknowledge their discomfort. Praise them as much as possible when their actions move in the right direction. Let teachers know it is acceptable to feel confused or somewhat overwhelmed with implementing the new change. Assure them that change takes time and patience. Please take steps to boost morale and remind people that they each contribute to the change initiative's success.

When the individual moves into the "new beginnings" phase, excitement and optimism build about the future and the success of the new initiative. Teacher skills grow, and comfort with the new way of doing things returns as teachers grow in self-confidence and competence. Teachers are likely to experience openness and higher energy levels. They can point to some early wins due to implementing the new innovation.

Continue to help teachers recognize their successes, but remember that not everyone will reach the new beginnings point simultaneously. Also, remember that the changes are not cemented into practice as of this state. People can still slip back to their old way of working if support and positive reinforcement are not provided to these individuals.

Levels of Use Theory

After you have developed a working relationship with your teachers, it is helpful to identify the level of innovation use for each of the teachers you support. Understanding their proficiency in implementing effective practices will help you know how to guide and provide the right amount of support for each teacher you will be working with on a regular basis.

To move an individual forward in their proficiency with a specific practice or a new innovation, it is essential to identify their starting level of proficiency. Loucks, Newlove & Hall (1975) identified eight levels of use that individuals might display when a new innovation is introduced in an organization. There are five levels of use where the innovation is being tried to varying degrees and three levels of "nonuse" of the innovation.

Level 0 is nonuse. Level 0 users know little or nothing about an innovation or change, and they show no behaviors that can be identified with the innovation or change. Since this individual isn't interested in the innovation or change, it can be challenging to work with this individual until you have been able to develop some interest on their part in knowing more about the innovation or change. You must first develop that critical personal relationship with the individual to make progress. A supportive relationship will help you provide a level 0 user with a way to connect their current practice to the intended innovation or change.

The next level of nonuse (level I) of an innovation is the "orientation" stage. During this stage, the individual may have heard about the new innovation, attended an orientation meeting to hear about it, read some display materials, or heard another group of teachers talking about the innovation. Their curiosity is piqued, but they have not yet decided to adopt the new innovation. It is essential to help level 1 users get their questions answered and to provide helpful information about the innovation. This approach will continue to build interest in the individual so they will be willing to learn more.

As discussed, success and feelings of self-empowerment are essential to turn a nonuser into a user. The level II nonuser has consciously decided to try to learn or use the new innovation. This is referred to as the "preparation" stage.

In some districts, the individual may have been told by the principal or the district that they must use the new approach, so no matter how reluctantly, the person is making plans to comply. The individual is not yet a user but is open to taking the first steps. As a coach, you must determine the best first step for the person to ensure they can be as successful as possible as early efforts are made.

Once the individual actively tries to use the new innovation or change, they move to level III, the "mechanical" user stage. In this stage, the individual focuses on short-term, day-to-day practices and has little time for reflection. The individual attempts to "do everything right" and make the new ideas or strategies work for themselves.

The coach can help the teacher organize lesson plans, find materials, and provide tips and suggestions, mainly when glitches occur. They can also help the teacher manage the new innovation as successfully and comfortably as possible.

The next level of use is level IVA, referred to as "routine" use. During this phase, the innovation is stabilized. The user has been given adequate time and assistance and has achieved a consistent and manageable way of working with new ideas or strategies. Many individuals in this level of use are happy with their practice. They are reluctant to refine their practice with more significant improvements.

The coach must compare the performance to the "highly effective" state of the innovation and provide support and encouragement to allow the individual to move to greater and more effective use of the innovation or change.

When a routine user acknowledges that they want to improve and strengthen their routines and common practices, they move to level IVB or the "refinement" stage of use. During the refinement stage, the teacher has a good command of the innovation and seeks to deepen the impact of what they are doing with instruction.

During this time, the coach may take the teacher to observe other teachers operating at a more advanced level, examine student work samples with the teacher, or do a model lesson to demonstrate more effective techniques that the teacher can incorporate into their repertoire.

The user is in the "integration" phase during level V usage. Teachers in this phase often talk about their work with the coach and their other grade-level peers. They listen to ideas and suggestions and then actively combine the ideas and strategies of others into their own practice. They are constantly experimenting to refine and improve their professional practice with the innovation. The user is actively asking questions and attempting to identify best practices that can make learning more effective for their students.

At this stage, the coach can begin a gradual release of coaching and attend to individuals still operating at the lower levels of use. The coach can still provide information, such as articles on refinements, that might interest the individual. The need for classroom support and encouragement is no longer a priority. Occasional visits to observe the person at this level may give the coach additional ideas to help less-proficient teachers. The coach may use this person as a model for teachers operating at the lower levels of use.

If the district or school requires fidelity to the program being implemented, there is more urgency to implement specific changes. The coach may have to remind users at this level of implementation why the innovation uses the specific strategies or components that it does to be effective.

In rare cases, if the teacher has gone too far afield from fidelity to the innovation, conversations with the evaluator may be required to refocus the teacher's use of the innovation appropriately. Remember that this action should only be undertaken when the coach has exhausted all their efforts to refocus the teacher's practice without administrator involvement.

The last level of use is level VI, or the "renewal" level. This level is where most coaches are probably operating and teachers who may have used the innovation before the adoption of the innovation in that school or grade level. Teachers at this level can provide professional development or serve as observers to provide feedback to other less proficient users. During this phase, the teacher constantly looks for new ideas to make them more effective.

Identifying the level of use of various teachers with whom you work can help you identify the logical next steps for each person. It will also help you to identify when to provide more and less support for your coachee.

Building Innovation Independence

As a coach, you must help teachers constantly reflect on the most important aspects of teaching. The four questions that we want teachers to ask themselves are:

1) "What are students currently able to do?"

2) "What is the next level of performance I want from my students?"

3) "How will I know when my students can perform at this level?" and,

4) "What type of instruction will help move my students to the next level of understanding?"

When teachers are constantly reflecting on these four questions as they plan their lessons, they will be operating at an independent level. As coaches, we can help our teachers reach this level of independence by being a sounding board to ask, "What can students do now as a result of your instruction that they could not do before?" These ideas must then be tied tightly to grade-level standards and benchmarks. Focused and precise instruction helps teachers be more effective with their students.

A quote attributed to Buddha says, "When the student is ready, the teacher will appear." As adult learners, we only hear what we are ready to hear. We must remember that if an individual is not ready to receive the new information, no matter how sound the advice is, it will likely not impact the other person.

If our coachees do not see the benefit of reaching a goal or expanding their skills in a new way, moving that person toward that end will be difficult. They may be stuck as a "nonuser" or as a "routine" user and never be able to move to more independent levels.

Listen carefully to what your teachers say and feel about an improvement you suggest. Understanding their beliefs will help determine their proximal development stage and use level. Help them feel competent, capable, and in control. Like I had to do with my teacher friend, Dan, you must begin where your teacher makes a connection and then move forward from that point. When you do, your teachers will appreciate your help.

As you move teachers toward proficiency, you can turn more of your attention to the new teachers who will arrive in your building each year or those still struggling with lower levels of use.

Giving Feedback to Enable Change

Feedback on the teacher's performance is essential for motivation and personal growth. Positive feedback fills our human need to be valued. Constructive feedback is very effective when it is timely, specific and builds on other strengths.

There are two components to feedback. One is the content or message that you want to share. The other speaks to the importance and value of the relationship. Effective feedback is respectful and helps the listener be self-reflective rather than defensive about the suggestions they are being given.

Some reflective questions that might help teachers think about their own practice are: "How is this different from..."; "What do you think would happen if..."; "What changes might you need to make…"; "What might be a good way to…"; "I am wondering if you noticed any gaps in…"; "What did students learn better with this activity than they had with the previous way you taught it?" and similar types of statements.

Since you have been chosen by someone in your district to serve in a coaching role, you likely already have some effective skills in working with others and establishing positive and supportive relationships with your peers

If you would like to learn more about building strong collaborative relationships or providing constructive feedback to your coachees, there are many helpful coaching books available on this topic where you can read more on these essential topics.

Conclusion

As you work with your teachers, help them make connections between what they already know and what they are learning. Just as we do with students, we scaffold adult learning from where they are at the present to the next higher level.

Help adult learners reflect on and identify goals for their own learning. Listen more than you talk, and help teachers reflect on their successes and challenges as much as possible. It will be more meaningful if these insights come from them rather than from you.

Once goals are determined, and you clearly understand the teacher's learning goals, model, provide guided practice and then begin the gradual release of support as the teacher becomes more comfortable and confident in the new skills.

Try to reduce feelings of stress and isolationism by building collegial and collaborative relationships. Ensure good communication with your coachee to reduce resistance as much as possible.

Think about the human needs that we discussed earlier in this chapter. When these needs are met, we are more likely to have a sense of optimism and efficacy. We all must feel competent, helpful, and in control of our situation. We all want to feel we belong and are part of meaningful work.

Remember that, as noted change experts Hall & Hord (2006) say, "Change is a process, not an event." Change takes time and moves more in spurts and starts than in a smooth, flowing manner. However, forward movement is still "forward movement," no matter how small.

Celebrate progress and small wins with your coachee whenever you can. Just as teachers can take pride in the accomplishments of their students, coaches can also take pride in the accomplishments and success of their peers - one teacher at a time.

Coaching Resources

K-3 Teacher – Coach Planning Survey –

Effective Literacy Environments

Please place an X in the appropriate box to rank each characteristic from 1 (needs work) to 3 (adequate) to 5 (very strong)

Environmental Traits	1	2	3	4	5
1. Does the classroom have a warm, open and inviting feeling when you enter the room and do students appear to feel safe, relaxed and self-confident?					
2. Does the teacher clearly exhibit a love of reading and model an enjoyment of reading him/herself?					
3. Does a high amount of talk take place in the classroom throughout the day from not only the teacher but among children as well? Do children seem to be enjoying talking and interacting with their teacher and with one another?					
4. Do students work together in fluid pairs, triads or small groups on a regular basis?					
5. Is there an abundance of easily accessible, age-appropriate fiction and non-fiction books present in the classroom? Does the classroom contain other print elements such as magazines, newspapers, labels, catalogs, signs, charts, and word rich bulletin boards?					
6. Are there charts with lists, recipes, songs, poems and communications, etc., around the room where children can read and work with them?					

Environmental Traits	1	2	3	4	5
7. Are print and images representative of the cultures and races of student populations readily visible in the classroom?					
8. Do both students and teacher display their natural curiosity during the day? Are students and teacher smiling most of the time and do they appear to be enjoying what they are doing?					

K-3 Teacher – Coach Planning Survey –

Effective Reading Instruction

Please place an X in the appropriate box to rank each characteristic
from 1 (needs work) to 3 (adequate) to 5 (very strong)

Reading Components in a Literacy Rich Classroom	1	2	3	4	5
1. Does the teacher prepare students for reading by activating student background knowledge prior to reading? Are concepts clarified with examples and/or illustrations so that children can link concepts to a familiar frame of reference?					
2. Are children encouraged to make observations, ask questions and link their own background knowledge to new learning on a frequent basis? Does the teacher link new concepts with examples or illustrations (both visual and verbal) on a regular basis?					
3. Does the teacher use many genres of reading in the classroom and often repeats student favorites on a regular basis?					

Reading Components in a Literacy Rich Classroom	1	2	3	4	5
4. Does the teacher encourage children to read and write throughout the school day? Are there opportunities for authentic and purposeful reading and writing?					
5. Does the teacher use anticipatory questions or picture walks to introduce new books and does s/he ask students to regularly make predictions before and during reading?					
6. Does the K-1 teacher use read aloud time to instruct students on the concepts of print such as directionality, handling of books, and various text elements such as title, author, illustrator, etc.? Does the 1-3rd grade teacher use read aloud time to discuss concepts such as author, illustrator, title page and story elements?					
7. Does the teacher use shared reading to reinforce reading skills and flexibly group and regroup students regularly according to instructional need?					
8. Does the teacher make use of appropriate technology to promote student interest and excitement in reading?					
9. Does the teacher use appropriate assessments and regular observations to guide student needs, guided reading work and flexible grouping practices?					

Reading Components in a Literacy Rich Classroom	1	2	3	4	5
10. Do struggling readers have additional support within the classroom to help them close the gap between their current performance level and grade level expectations? [Does the school have Tier 2 and Tier 3 RtI support for those who need more intensive help? If so, does the teacher make use of these supports to ensure early literacy success?]					
Phonemic Awareness and Phonics					
1. Does the teacher use oral activities such as rhyming, word play and the manipulation of words, syllables and sounds?					
2. Does the teacher use engaging activities and materials such as hand motions, clapping, Elkonin boxes, letter tiles and other manipulatives to help students understand sound-symbol relationships?					
3. Does the teacher progress from the easier phonemic awareness activities to the more difficult concepts such as blending, segmenting, isolating and phoneme manipulation?					
4. Does the teacher use a systematic phonics program for grades K-2 (and students in K-3 who still need these concepts) to ensure that all students have appropriate foundational skills for word recognition?					
5. Does the teacher help students understand phonemes in all positions in words (initial, final, and medial) and teach students to manipulate onset and rime?					

Reading Components in a Literacy Rich Classroom	1	2	3	4	5
11. Does the teacher involve students as appropriate in activities to build and enhance letter recognition, sound-symbol correspondence, and develop phonemic awareness and an understanding of basic phonics rules?					
12. Does the teacher use big books to reinforce phonemic awareness, the concepts of letter, word and sentence and to reinforce sound-symbol correspondence? Are big books placed in shared areas for student access?					
13. Does the teacher use a variety of book types such as big books, predictable books, alphabet books, controlled text, trade books, fiction and nonfiction as may be appropriate to the grade level? Does the K-1 teacher use predictable books and pattern books to reinforce phonemic awareness concepts?					
Fluency Development					
1. Does the teacher model good verbal expression, speed, accuracy and prosody while reading?					
2. Does the teacher provide feedback to students to help them improve their own fluency skills?					
3. Does the K-1 teacher read aloud to students on a daily basis? Are there several oral read aloud times occurring during the day both during reading class as well as during other content subjects in 2nd and 3rd grade classrooms?					

Reading Components in a Literacy Rich Classroom	1	2	3	4	5
4. Does the teacher use oral language activities such as songs, finger plays, rhyme, chants, choral reading, echo reading, Reader's Theater and poetry as age appropriate on a regular basis to enhance and build oral language skills?					
Vocabulary Development					
1. Does the teacher use a rich and varied vocabulary with plenty of opportunities for students to link new words to a visual representation such as an object, realia or a picture?					
2. Is there a word wall visible and is not only present but used to practice and learn new words on a regular basis? Are there content word walls in 2-3rd grade classrooms to help students learn specialized vocabulary?					
3. Does the teacher assist students with challenging words and provides pictures, examples or connections to already known concepts as needed?					
4. Does the teacher work to increase the student's storehouse of words recognized automatically by sight?					
5. Does the teacher introduce words of high utility and help students develop automaticity with these words?					

Reading Components in a Literacy Rich Classroom	1	2	3	4	5
6. Does the teacher provide students with explicit strategies to identify unknown words such as using the context, using word parts and so forth?					
Comprehension and Higher Order Reading					
1. Does the teacher provide ample time for students to engage in reading (i.e. independent reading time, paired reading time, repeated readings, literature circles)? Are kindergarten students able to explore "blessed" books on a regular and independent basis?					
2. Does the teacher help the students connect to their own prior knowledge before reading (i.e. discussions, predictions, realia, pictures, etc.)?					
3. Does the teacher provide sufficient guided practice in decodable words? Does the teacher provide opportunities for students to blend and read words in context?					
4. During reading, are children are asked to make predictions or draw inferences on a frequent basis?					
5. Is there adequate time given for students to voice their thoughts, their ideas and ask questions about text and what they are reading?					

Reading Components in a Literacy Rich Classroom	1	2	3	4	5
6. Are there opportunities for children to participate in analytic conversations with peers including making inferences, drawing conclusions, making predictions, asking questions, retelling and summarizing and making connections from text to self, text to text and text to world on a routine basis?					
7. Does the teacher help students visualize scenes or characters via description or drawing?					
8. Does the teacher explicitly teach students how to read and interpret graphs, diagrams and charts within text?					
9. Do classroom projects and activities allow children to work at higher levels such as application, analysis, evaluation or synthesis?					
10. Does the teacher ask students to explain their thinking and does the teacher model his/her own thinking orally for the students on a frequent basis?					
11. Does the teacher help students sequence important events in the story on a regular basis?					
12. Are children asked to draw inferences or make conclusions on a frequent basis?					
13. Is adequate time provided to students to voice their thoughts, ideas and to ask questions about what they are reading or listening to during reading time?					

Reading Components in a Literacy Rich Classroom	1	2	3	4	5
14. Does the teacher stress higher order questions more than literal or knowledge and application level questions and guide students to deeper levels of thought before, during and after reading?					
Connecting Writing to Reading					
1. Is the teacher knowledgeable of ways to help students develop ideas, organization, content and voice in their writing?					
2. Is classroom writing reinforced through writing centers, teacher modeled writing and/or journals?					
3. Does the classroom not only promote reading but also writing by having many opportunities for students to engage in writing during the day?					

4-8 Teacher – Coach Planning Survey –

Effective Literacy Environments

Please place an X in the appropriate box to rank each characteristic from 1 (needs work) to 3 (adequate) to 5 (very strong)

Environmental Traits	1	2	3	4	5
1. Does the classroom have a warm, positive and supportive atmosphere in the room at all times?					
2. Does the room have a variety of different types and levels of books (i.e. fiction and non-fiction, high interest-low vocabulary, reference, audio books, magazines, comic books, online books) available to students?					
3. Is there an area where students can share book recommendations and reviews of reading materials?					
4. Is there a shared reading area for reading aloud or an individual reading area that students may use to relax and enjoy a book during independent reading time?					
5. Are there print materials and images representative of the cultures and races of classroom populations visible in the room?					
6. Is there an abundance of high-quality, literacy-related student work posted on the classroom walls and bulletin boards of the classroom?					
7. Do both students and teacher appear to enjoy one another's company and do students appear willing to take risks and do they display a relaxed, self-confidence when approaching tasks?					

4-8 Teacher – Coach Planning Survey –

Effective Reading Instruction

Please place an X in the appropriate box to rank each characteristic from 1 (needs work) to 3 (adequate) to 5 (very strong)

Reading Components in a Literacy Rich Classroom	1	2	3	4	5
1. Does the teacher help students reflect on their own reading habits and interests? Does the teacher provide opportunities for students to explore and grow as independent and capable readers?					
2. Does the teacher include a wide variety of text levels in the classroom?					
3. Does the teacher use both traditional or text-based readings as well as timely articles and/or contemporary fiction when appropriate for instruction?					
4. Does the teacher thoughtfully organize lessons to include before, during and after reading goals and strategies?					
5. Does the teacher help students set purposeful goals for content reading?					
6. Does the teacher flexibly group and regroup students according to instructional need?					
7. Does the teacher use appropriate assessments and regular observations to guide student needs, guided reading work and flexible grouping practices?					
8. Does the teacher provide support to build student self-confidence and increase reading stamina and persistence?					

Reading Components in a Literacy Rich Classroom	1	2	3	4	5
9. Do struggling readers have additional support within the classroom to help them close the gap between their current performance level and grade level expectations? Does the school have Tier 2 and Tier 3 RtI support for those who need more intensive help? If so, does the teacher make use of these supports to ensure early literacy success?					
10. Does the teacher make use of appropriate technology to promote student interest and excitement in reading?					
Vocabulary Development					
1. Is there evidence that word learning has a high priority in this classroom (i.e. evidence such as word walls, vocabulary graphic organizers or webs, word games, affixes and word part learning and learning the "shades of meaning" of words)?					
2. Does the teacher assist students with challenging words and provide pictures, examples or connections to already known concepts as needed?					
3. Has the teacher abandoned "assign, define, test" in favor of using strategies like graphic organizers, word splashes and other vocabulary enhancing techniques to help students learn new concepts and key vocabulary?					
4. Do students learn word identification and affixes (chunks, roots, prefixes, suffixes, bases), word origins and how to break words into component parts to analyze and determine meanings?					

222

Reading Components in a Literacy Rich Classroom	1	2	3	4	5
5. Do content teachers use content learning journals to highlight relevant vocabulary and to document and extend content learning?					
6. Does the teacher help students approach new words systematically and logically?					
7. Does the teacher actively work to increase the students speaking, listening, reading and writing vocabularies?					
8. Does the teacher help students become familiar with specialized vocabulary, phrases and idioms used in various disciplines and discourses?					
Fluency Development					
1. Does the teacher help students locate independent reading texts that align with student abilities and interests?					
2. Does the 4-6th grade teacher (or remedial teacher in 7-8) use oral techniques such as echo reading, choral reading, repeated readings or Reader's Theater passages to strengthen fluency and oral reading skills?					
3. Does the teacher use flexible shared reading groups to reinforce reading skills?					
4. Does the teacher eliminate round robin reading in favor of silent, partner or small group reading techniques?					
5. Does the teacher help students learn how to increase silent reading speed while maintaining accuracy?					

Reading Components in a Literacy Rich Classroom	1	2	3	4	5
Comprehension and Higher Order Thinking					
1. Does the teacher help the students connect to their own prior knowledge before reading (i.e. discussions, making predictions, anticipation guides, word splashes, etc.)?					
2. Does the teacher help students visualize scenes or characters via description or drawing?					
3. Does the teacher help students make predictions and/or generate questions based on the content and structure of the text?					
4. Does the teacher help students use graphic organizers to see relationships and connections?					
5. Does the teacher help students identify story elements, retell the main idea and supporting details and sequence important events in the story on a regular basis?					
6. Is there evidence that Language Arts teachers use journals or in text notes to record personal experiences and connections as they are reading? Do content teachers teach students to use a consistent (preferably school-wide) note-taking method and ask students to use in text notes to identify areas of confusion?					
7. Does the teacher help students make connections to themselves, to other texts they have read and to the world around them while reading?					
8. Does the teacher guide students to deeper levels of thought through reflective and open-ended questions?					

Reading Components in a Literacy Rich Classroom	1	2	3	4	5
9. Does the teacher concentrate on helping students increase comprehension after reading by emphasizing higher order skills such as summarizing, comparing and contrasting, sequencing, making inferences, analyzing and synthesizing information?					
10. Do the students have opportunities to extend learning with activities that require higher order thinking, be involved in in-depth projects, book studies and/or literature circles as appropriate to the discipline?					
11. Does the teacher develop student's metacognitive skills by asking students to explain their thinking on a regular basis and does the teacher model his/her own thinking for students on an ongoing basis?					
12. Does the teacher help students summarize, compare and contrast, categorize, synthesize and organize textual information from multiple sources both orally and in writing?					
13. Does the teacher help students identify appropriate content reading skills including summarizing and applying "fix-up" strategies when meaning is lost?					
14. Does the teacher help the students understand the rhetorical context of the text (i.e. audience, purpose, arguments, social-political connections)?					

Reading Components in a Literacy Rich Classroom	1	2	3	4	5
Connecting Writing to Reading					
1. Are students often asked to reflect on their reading both orally and in writing?					
2. Do teachers help students paraphrase and interpret texts in writing?					
3. Do teachers help students write from a particular point of view and use appropriate voice for the writing audience?					
4. Is the teacher knowledgeable of ways to help students develop ideas, organize content, create variety in sentence structure and use explicit vocabulary in writing?					
5. Does the teacher regularly conference with students on reading and writing performance? Do content teachers help students express themselves in authentic types of writing consistent with the content discipline?					
6. Is writing reinforced in the classroom through writing centers, teacher modeled writing and/or journals? Do content teachers ask students to reflect on their learning through content journals or reflective writing?					
7. Is there evidence that students use the writing process on an ongoing basis to different stages of refinement to create content of all types in the classroom?					

9-12 Teacher – Coach Planning Survey –
Effective Literacy Environments

Please place an X in the appropriate box to rank each characteristic from 1 (needs work) to 3 (adequate) to 5 (very strong)

Environmental Traits	1	2	3	4	5
1. Does the classroom have a warm, positive and supportive atmosphere in the room at all times?					
2. Does the English classroom have a variety of different types and levels of books (i.e. fiction and non-fiction, high interest-low vocabulary, reference, audio, magazines, comic books online books) available to students?					
3. Is there an area where students can share book recommendations and reviews?					
4. Does the content classroom have a variety of different types of books and articles (both traditional and contemporary) that align to instructional content topics and are written at various reading levels?					
5. Are there print materials and images representative of the cultures and races of classroom populations visible in the room?					
6. Does the teacher explore student interests and include a variety of resources beyond the core textbook?					
7. Is there an abundance of high-quality, student work posted on the classroom walls and bulletin boards of the classroom?					
8. Do both students and teacher appear to enjoy one another's company? Do students appear willing to take risks and do they display a relaxed, self-confidence when approaching tasks?					

9-12 Teacher – Coach Planning Survey –

Effective Reading Instruction

Please place an X in the appropriate box to rank each characteristic from 1 (needs work) to 3 (adequate) to 5 (very strong)

Reading Components in a Literacy Rich Classroom	1	2	3	4	5
1. Does the teacher help students reflect on their own reading habits and interests? Does the teacher provide opportunities for students to explore and grow as independent and capable readers?					
2. Does the teacher include a wide variety of text levels in the classroom?					
3. Does the content teacher use traditional or text-based readings as well as timely articles and/or contemporary fiction when appropriate for instruction?					
4. Does the teacher thoughtfully organize lessons to include before, during and after reading goals and strategies?					
5. Does the teacher help students set purposeful goals for content reading and for learning?					
6. Does the teacher provide some choice in work projects and flexibly group and regroup students according to instructional need?					
7. Does the teacher use appropriate assessments and regular observations to guide student needs and instructional practices?					
8. Does the teacher provide support to build student self-confidence and increase reading stamina and persistence?					

Reading Components in a Literacy Rich Classroom	1	2	3	4	5
9. Do struggling readers have additional support within the classroom to help them close the gap between their current performance level and grade level expectations? Does the school have Tier 2 and Tier 3 RtI support for those who need more intensive help? If so, does the teacher make use of these supports to ensure early literacy success?					
10. Does the teacher make use of appropriate technology to promote student interest and excitement in reading?					
Vocabulary Development					
1. Is there evidence that word learning has a high priority in this classroom (i.e. evidence such as word walls, vocabulary graphic organizers or webs, word games, affixes and word part learning and learning the "shades of meaning" of words)?					
2. Does the teacher assist students with challenging words and provide pictures, examples or connections to already known concepts as needed?					
3. Has the teacher abandoned "assign, define, test" in favor of strategies like graphic organizers, word splashes and other vocabulary enhancing techniques to help students learn new concepts and key vocabulary?					
4. Do students learn word identification and affixes (chunks, roots, prefixes, suffixes, bases), word origins and how to break words into component parts to analyze and determine meanings?					

Reading Components in a Literacy Rich Classroom	1	2	3	4	5
5. Do content teachers use content learning journals to highlight relevant vocabulary and to document and extend content learning?					
6. Does the teacher help students approach new words systematically and logically?					
7. Does the teacher actively work to increase the students speaking, listening, reading and writing vocabularies?					
8. Does the teacher help students become familiar with specialized vocabulary, phrases and idioms used in various disciplines and discourses?					
Fluency Development					
1. Does the teacher help students locate independent reading texts that align with student abilities and interests?					
2. When high numbers of remedial students are present in the classroom room, does the teacher use oral techniques such choral reading, repeated readings or Reader's Theater passages to strengthen fluency and build oral fluency and reading skills?					
3. Does the teacher use flexible shared reading groups to reinforce reading skills?					
4. Does the teacher eliminate round robin reading in favor of silent, partner or small group reading techniques?					

Reading Components in a Literacy Rich Classroom	1	2	3	4	5
Comprehension and Higher Order Thinking					
1. Does the teacher help the students connect to their own prior knowledge before reading (i.e. discussions, making predictions, anticipation guides, word splashes, etc.)?					
2. Does the English teacher help students visualize scenes or characters via description or drawing?					
3. Does the teacher help students make predictions and/or generate questions based on the content and structure of the text?					
4. Does the teacher help students use graphic organizers to see relationships and connections?					
5. Does the teacher help students identify story elements, retell the main idea and supporting details and sequence important events in the story on a regular basis?					
6. Is there evidence that Language Arts teachers use journals or in text notes to record personal experiences and connections as they are reading? Do content teachers teach students to use a consistent (preferably school-wide) note-taking method and ask students to use in-text notes to identify areas of confusion?					
7. Does the teacher help students make connections to themselves, to other texts they have read and to the world around them while reading?					
8. Does the teacher guide students to deeper levels of thought through reflective and open-ended questions?					

Reading Components in a Literacy Rich Classroom	1	2	3	4	5
9. Does the teacher concentrate on helping students increase comprehension after reading by emphasizing higher order skills such as summarizing, comparing and contrasting, sequencing, making inferences, analyzing and synthesizing information?					
10. Do the students have opportunities to extend learning with activities that require higher order thinking, be involved in in-depth projects, book studies and/or literature circles as appropriate to the discipline?					
11. Does the teacher develop student's metacognitive skills by asking students to explain their thinking on a regular basis and does the teacher model his/her own thinking for students on an ongoing basis?					
12. Does the teacher help students summarize, compare and contrast, categorize, synthesize and organize textual information from multiple sources both orally and in writing?					
13. Does the teacher help students identify appropriate content reading skills including summarizing and applying "fix-up" strategies when meaning is lost?					
14. Does the teacher help the students understand the rhetorical context of the text (i.e. audience, purpose, arguments, social-political connections)?					

Reading Components in a Literacy Rich Classroom	1	2	3	4	5
Connecting Writing to Reading					
1. Are students often asked to reflect on their reading both orally and in writing?					
2. Do teachers help students paraphrase and interpret texts in writing?					
3. Do teachers help students write from a particular point of view and use appropriate voice for the writing audience?					
4. Is the teacher knowledgeable of ways to help students develop ideas, organize content, create variety in sentence structure and use explicit content related vocabulary in writing?					
5. Does the English teacher regularly conference with students on writing performance? Do content teachers help students express themselves in authentic types of writing consistent with the content discipline?					
6. Is writing reinforced in the classroom through teacher modeled writing and/or journals? Do content teachers ask students to reflect on their learning through content journals or reflective writing?					
7. Is there evidence that students use the writing process on an ongoing basis to different stages of refinement to create content of all types in the English classroom?					

Guided Reading Survey – K-5

Guided Reading K-5	1	2	3	4	5
1. Does the teacher provide a daily guided reading experience for each child for a minimum of 15-20 minutes for K-2 and 20-30 minutes for grades 3-5?					
2. Does the teacher regularly assess and reassess student's reading needs either formally or informally?					
3. Does the teacher group and regroup students by instructional needs?					
4. Does the teacher understand how to assess the readability and skill level of text and select "just right" texts for the needs of students in the guided reading groups?					
5. Does the teacher provide focused time on task for students to practice needed skills?					
6. Does the teacher introduce the text by connecting with student's background knowledge or asking students to make predictions about the text?					
7. Does the teacher clarify any unusual vocabulary or provide explanations about new or unusual words that may occur in the text?					
8. During guided reading time, does the teacher model short mini-lessons as may be needed to access the text features or learn appropriate reading strategies?					
9. During guided reading time, does the teacher provide supportive and specific feedback to students when oral reading to improve performance?					

Guided Reading K-5	1	2	3	4	5
10. After reading, does the teacher help students clarify understandings and make connections to their own ideas and experiences that relate to the text?					
11. After reading, does the teacher ask students to summarize the text, sequence key events or respond to higher-level questions about what they have read?					
12. During guided reading time does the teacher provide enough structure and organization to allow children who are not participating in the guided reading group to work independently or in structured learning centers so as not to distract other students or the teacher from his or her guided reading group?					
13. Are learning centers targeted to student instructional needs and well organized to allow students to independently complete the center tasks?					
14. Does the teacher make notes on each child's performance during guided reading groups to assess progress, guide future instruction and record progress?					
15. Does the teacher sometimes ask the students to reflect on their reading either orally or in writing?					

Predictable Pattern and Alliterative Books for K-3 Classrooms

Alborough, Jess	Duck in the Truck
Aliki	My Five Senses
Arma, Tom	We're Going on Safari
Astley, Judy	When One Cat Woke Up
Baer, Gene	Thump, Thump, rat-a-tat-tat
Barton, Byron	Dinosaurs, Dinosaurs
Bergman, Mara	Snip Snap! What is That?
Blackstone, Stella	Alligator Alphabet
Brandenberg, Franz	Aunt Nina, Good Night
Brown, Margaret Wise	Goodnight Moon
Cabrera, Jane	Ten in a Bed
Carle, Eric	The Grouchy Ladybug
Carle, Eric	The Very Hungary Caterpillar
Cuyler, Margery	That's Good! That's Bad!
Dewdney, Anna	Llama, Llama Mad at Mama
Dewdney, Anna	Llama, Llama, Red Pajama
Emberly, Ed	Klippity Klop
Gill, Janie S.	Dreams
Gill, Janie S.	Freddy the Frog
Gill, Janie S.	Can a Fox Wear Polka-Dotted Socks?
Gilman, Phoebe	Something for Nothing
Guarino, Deborah	Is Your Mama a Llama?
Hutchins, Pat	Bumpety Bump!
Jonas, Ann	Color Dance
Joose, Barbara	Mama, Do You Love Me?
Krause, Robert	Whose Mouse Are You?

Lewis, Kevin	Chugga Chugga Choo-Choo
Martin, Bill	Brown Bear, Brown Bear
Martin, Bill	Chicka Chicka Sticka Sticka
Martin, Bill	Panda Bear, Panda Bear
Martin, Bill	Polar Bear, Polar Bear
Martin, Bill	Chicka Chicka Boom Boom
Numeroff, Laura J.	If You Give a Moose a Muffin
Numeroff, Laura J.	If You Give a Mouse a Cookie
Numeroff, Laura J.	If You Give a Pig a Pancake
Parker, John	I Love Spiders
Peek, Merle	Mary Wore Her Red Dress
Polacco, Patricia	Oh, Look!
Prelutsky, Jack	Random House Book of Poetry for
Children	
Roffey, Maureen	Spy at the Zoo
Seeger, Pete	Abiyoyo
Spence, Robert	Clickey Clack
Ward, Leila	I am Eyes – Ni Macho
Wells, Rosemary	Noisy Nora
William, Bee	And the Train Goes…

References

Allington, R. (2001). *What Really Matters for Struggling Readers*. New York, NY:
Addison Wesley Educational Publishers Inc.

Alvermann, D.E., Phelps, S.F., & Ridgeway, V.G. (2007). *Content Area Reading and Literacy*, 5th Edition. Boston, MA: Pearson Education.

Anders, P.L., & Evens, K.S. (1994). Relationship Between Teachers' Beliefs and Their Instructional Practice in Reading. In *Beliefs About Text and Instruction with Text*, Garner, R. and Alexander, P. (Eds.), (pp.137-54). Hillsdale, NJ: Lawrence Erlbaum.

Annenberg Institute for School Reform (2004). Instructional Coaching:
Professional Development Strategies That Improve Instruction. The Annenberg Institute for School Reform. Providence, RI.

Baker, S. K., Simmons, D. C., & Kameenui, E. J. (1995). *Vocabulary acquisition: Synthesis of the research* (Tech. Rep. No. 13). National Center to Improve the Tools of Educators, University of Oregon, Eugene, OR.

Bauman, J.F., Kameenui, E.J., & Ash, G.E. (2003). Research on vocabulary instruction: Voltaire redux. In J. Flood, D. Lapp, J.R. Squire, & J.M. Jensen (Eds.), *Handbook on research on teaching the English language arts* (2nd edition, (pp.752-785). Mahwah, NJ: Earlbaum.

Baumann, J. F., & Kameenui, E. J. (1991). Research on vocabulary instruction: Ode to Voltaire. In J. Flood, J. J. D. Lapp, & J. R. Squire (Eds.), *Handbook of research on teaching the English language arts*. 604-632. New York: MacMillan.

Beach, R., Anson, C., Kastman Breuch, L., & Swiss, T. (2009). *Teaching Writing Using Blogs, Wikis, and Other Digital Tools.* Norwood, MA: Christopher-Gordon Publishers, Inc.

Bean, R.M. (2004). *The Reading Specialist: Leadership for the classroom, school, and community.* New York, NY: Guilford Press.

Bean, R.M. & Wilson, R. (1981). *Effecting change in school reading programs: The resource Role.* Newark, DE: International Reading Association.

Beyer, B. K. (1991). *Teaching thinking skills: A handbook for elementary school teachers.* Boston: Allyn and Bacon.

Blachman, B. A. (1991). An alternative classroom reading program for learning disabled and other low-achieving children. In Ellis (Ed.), *Intimacy with Language: A Forgotten Basic in Teacher Education.* (pp.49-55). Baltimore, MD: Orton Dyslexia Society.

Blevins, W. (1998). *Phonics from A to Z: A practical guide.* New York, NY: Scholastic Professional Books.

Bos, C. S., & Anders, P. L. (1990). Effects of interactive vocabulary instruction on the vocabulary learning and reading comprehension of junior-high learning-disabled students. *Learning Disability Quarterly, 13* (1), 31-42.

Bridges, W. (1991). *Managing transitions: Making the most of change.* Reading, MA: Addison-Wesley.

Brown, A.L., Palincsar, A.S., & Purcell, L. (1986). Poor readers: Teach, don't label. In Neisser (Ed.). *The school achievement of minority children: New perspectives.* (pp.105-143). Hillsdale, N.J.: Erlbaum.

Casey, K. (2006). *Literacy Coaching: The Essentials.* Portsmouth, NH: Heinemann.

Clay, M.M. (1972). *The Early Detection of Reading Difficulties.* Auckland, NZ: Heinemann.

Clay, M.M. (1991). *Becoming Literate: The Construction of Control.* Portsmouth, NH: Heinemann.

Clay, M.M. (2006). *An Observation Survey of Early Literacy Achievement.* (2nd Edition), Portsmouth, NH: Heinemann.

Combs, M. (1994). Implementing a Holistic Reading Series in First Grade: Experiences with a Conversation Group. *Reading Horizons* 34 (3): 196-207.

Cunningham, A.E., & Stanovich, K.E. (1998). What reading does for the mind. *American Educator*, 22 (Spring/Summer), 8-15.

Darling-Hammond, L. (1997). School Reform at the Crossroads: Confronting the Central Issues of Teaching. *Educational Policy* 11(2); 151-166.

Darling-Hammond, L. (2000). Teacher quality and student achievement: A review of state policy evidence. *Educational Policy Analysis Archives*, 8(1). Retrieved May 31, 2008, from https://epaa.asu.edu/epaa/v8n1/.

Darling-Hammond, L. & Richardson, Nikole (2009). Research Review – Teacher Learning: What Matters? How Teachers Learn. Vol. 66:5. Pgs. 46-53.

Dickinson, D.K., & Tabors, P.O. (2001). *Beginning Literacy with Language.* Baltimore, MD: Brookes Publishing.

Dozier, C. (2006). *Responsive Literacy Coaching: Tools for Creating and Sustaining Purposeful Change.* Portland, ME: Stenhouse Publishers.

Durkin, D. (1966). *Children Who Read Early.* New York, NY: Teachers College Press.

Ehren, B., Lenz, K., & Deshler, D. (2004). Enhancing literacy proficiency with adolescents and young adults, In Stone et al., (Ed.) *Handbook of Language and Literacy.* New York, NY: Guilford Press.

Francis, D.J., Shaywitz, S.E., Stuebing, K.K., Shaywitz, B.A., & Fletcher, J.M. (1996). Developmental lag versus deficit models of reading disability: A longitudinal, individual growth curves analysis. *Journal of Educational Psychology*, 88(1), 3-17.

Frayer, D.A., Frederick, W.C., & Klausmeier, H.G. (1969). *A science for testing the level of concept mastery* (Working paper No. 16). Madison, WI: University of Wisconsin Research and Development Center for Cognitive Learning.

Friend, M.P., & Cook, L. (2003). *Interactions: Collaboration skills for school professionals*. Boston, MA: Allyn and Bacon.

Fullan, M. (1993). *Change Forces: Probing the Depth of Educational Reform*. New York, NY: Falmer Press.

Fullan, M. (2007). *The New Meaning of Educational Change*, 4th ed, New York, NY: Teachers College Press.

Fullan, M., & Hargreaves, A. (1992). *What's Worth Fighting For? Working Together for Your School*. Toronto: Elementary Teachers Federation of Ontario; New York, NY: Teachers College Press.

Fullan M. & Stiegelbauer, S. (1991). The new meaning of educational change. 2nd ed. New York, NY: Teachers College Press.

Gallimore, R., & Tharp, R. (1990). Teaching Mind in Society: teaching, schooling, and literate discourse. In Moll, L. (Ed.). *Vygotsky and Education: Instructional implications and applications of sociohistorical psychology*. New York, NY: Cambridge University Press.

Glasser, W. (1998). *Choice Theory in the Classroom*. New York, NY: Harper.

Hall, G.E., & Hord, S.M. (2006). *Implementing Change: Patterns, Principles, and Potholes*. New York, NY: Pearson.

Hall, S.L., & Moats, L.C. (1998). *Straight Talk About Reading*. New York, NY: McGraw-Hill.

Hart, B., & Risley, T.R. (1995). *Meaningful Differences in Everyday Experiences of Young American Children.* Baltimore, MD: Brookes Publishing.

Hart, B. & Risley, T. R. (2003). The early catastrophe: The 30-million-word gap by age 3. *American Educator,* (Spring). 4-9. Retrieved from https://www.aft.org/newspubs/periodicals/ae/spring2003/

Heber, H.L., & Nelson, J.B. (1986). Questioning is not the answer. In Dishner, E.K. et al. (Ed.), *Reading in the Content Areas: Improving classroom instruction,* (2nd ed., pp. 210-215). Dubuque, IA: Kendall-Hunt.

Hiebert, E.H., & Sawyer, C.C. (1984). *Young Children's Concurrent Abilities in Reading and Spelling.* Paper presented at the annual meeting of the American Educational Research Association. New Orleans, LA.

Iding, M.K., Cosby, M.E., & Speitel, T. (2002). Teachers and technology: Beliefs and practices. *International Journal of Instructional Media,* 29(2), 153-170.

Juel, C. (1988). Learning to read and write: A longitudinal study of 54 children from first through fourth grades. *Journal of Educational Psychology,* 80, 437-447.

Juel, C. (1991). Beginning reading. In R. Barr, M. L. Kamil, P.B. Mosenthal, and P.D. Pearson, (Eds.) *Handbook of Reading Research,* (Vol. 2, pp. 759-788). Mahwah, NJ: Lawrence Erlbaum.

Juel, C. (1994). *Learning to Read and Write in One Elementary School.* New York: Springer-Verlag.

Juel, C., & Roper-Schneider, D. (1985). The influence of basal readers on first-grade reading. *Reading Research Quarterly,* 20, 134-152.

Kamil, M. (2003). *Adolescents and Literacy: Reading for the 21st Century.* Washington, D.C.: Alliance for Excellent Education.

Knight, J. (2004). Instructional coaching. *StrateNotes* 13(3): 1-5. Lawrence, KS: University of Kansas, Center for Research on Learning. Retrieved May 31, 2008, from https://www.instructionalcoach.org/nov_stratenotes.pdf.

Kruidenier, J. (2002). Research-Based Principles for Adult Basic Education Reading Instruction. RMC Research Corporation, Portsmouth, N.H.

Lenhart, A., & Madden, M. (2007). *Social networking websites in teens: An overview.* Washington, DC: Pew Internet and American Life Project. Retrieved December 31, 2010, from https://www.pewinternet.org.

Lenhart, A., Sousan, A., Smith, A., & MacGill, A.R. (2008). *Writing, Technology, and Teens.* Washington, D.C: Pew Internet and American Life Project. April 24, Retrieved May 15, 2011, from https://www.pewinternet.org/~/media/Files/Reports/2008/PIP_Writing_Report_FINAL3.pdf.pdfV

Lindfors, J.W. (1987). *Children's Language and Learning,* 2nd ed. Englewood Cliffs, NJ: Prentice-Hall.

Loban, W. (1976). *Language Development: kindergarten through grade twelve,* Research Report no. 18. Urbana, IL: National Council of Teachers of English.

Loucks, S.F., Newlove, B. W., & Hall, G.E. (1975). *Measuring Levels of Use of the Innovation: A Manual for Trainers, Interviewers, and Raters.* Austin, TX: The University of Texas at Austin, Research and Development Center for Teacher Education.

Lyons, C.A., & Pinell, G.S. (2001). *Systems for Change in Literacy Education: A Guide to Professional Development.* Portsmouth, NH: Heinemann.

Marzano, R.J., Pickering, D.J., & Pollock, J.E. (2001). *Classroom Instruction That Works*, Alexandria, VA: Association of Supervision and Curriculum Development.

Marzano, R.J., & Pickering, D.J. (2005). *Building Academic Vocabulary: Teacher's Manual*. Alexandria, VA: ASCD.

McGinley, W. J., and Denner, P.R. (1987). *Story-impressions: A pre-reading-writing activity*. Journal of Reading, 31, 248-253.

Moats, L.C. (2000). *Speech to Print: Language Essentials for Teachers*. Baltimore, MD: Brookes Publishing.

Moore, M. (1991). Reflective Teaching and Learning Through the Use of Learning Logs. *Journal of Reading Education* 17, 35-49.

National Assessment of Educational Progress (NAEP) (2022). Results from
  the NAEP 2022 Civics & U.S. History Assessments at Grade 8 are here! National Center for Educational Statistics. Washington D.C.: https://nces.ed.gov/nationsreportcard/.

National Reading Panel Report (2000). *Teaching children to read: An evidence-based assessment of the scientific research literature on reading and its implications for reading instruction* (National Institute of Health Pub. No. 00-4754). Washington, D.C.: National Institute of Child Health and Human Development.

Neufeld, B., & Roper, D. (2003). *Coaching: A strategy for developing institutional capacity, promises, and practicalities*. Washington, DC: Aspen Institute Program on Education.

Oka, E., & Paris, S. (1985). Patterns of motivation and reading skills in underachieving children. In S. Ceci (Ed.), *Handbook of cognitive, social, and neuropsychological aspects of learning disabilities* (Vol. 2). Hillsdale, NJ: Erlbaum

Ogle, D. (1986). K-W-L: A teaching model that develops active reading of expository text. *The Reading Teacher*. 39, 564-570.

Opitz, M.F., & Rasinski, T. V. (1998). *Goodbye Round Robin: 25 Effective Oral Reading Strategies.* Portsmouth, NH: Heinemann.

Pang, E., & Kamil, M. (2003). *Updates and Extensions to the Teacher Education Research Database.* Presented to the American Education Research Association, March 2003. Chicago, Il.

Pearson, P.D., Roehler, L.R., Dole, J.A., & Duffy, G.G. (1992). Developing Expertise in Reading Comprehension. In Samuals, S.J. and Farstrup, A. (Eds.). *What Research Has to Say About Reading Instruction,* (2nd edition). Newark, DE: International Reading Association.

Raphael, T.E., Highfield, K., & Au, K.H. (2006*). QAR Now: A Powerful and Practical Framework That Develops Comprehension and Higher-Level Thinking in All Students (Theory and Practice).* New York, NY: Scholastic Publishers.

Rasinski, T., Flexer, C., & Boomgarden-Szypulski, T.A. (2006). Harebrain, Inc. Anoka, MN.

Rasinski, T. (2002). Speed Does Matter in Reading. The Reading Teacher. Vol. 54:2. Pgs. 146-151.

Readence, J.E., Baldwin, R.S., & Head, M.H. (1986). Direct instruction in processing metaphors. *Journal of Reading Behavior,* 18, 325-339.

Readence, J.E., Bean, T.W., & Baldwin, R.S., (1998). Dubuque, Iowa: Kendall/Hunt.

Reiss, K. (2007). *Leadership Coaching for Educators: Bringing out the best in school administrators.* Thousand Oaks, CA: Corwin Press.

Robbins, C., & Ehri, L.C. (1994). Reading storybooks to kindergartners helps them learn

New vocabulary words. *Journal of Educational Psychology* 86(1), pp 54-64.

Rodgers, E.M., & Pinell, G.S. (2002). *Learning from Teaching in Literacy Education: New Perspectives on Professional Development*. Portsmouth, NH: Heinemann.

Rosenholtz, S.J. (1991). *Teacher's workplace: The social organization of schools*. New York, New York: Teachers College Press.

Russo, A. (2004). *School-Based Coaching. Harvard Education Letter Research Online*. Retrieved May 30, 2008, from https://www.edletter.org/past/issues/2004-ja/coaching.shtml.

Sagor, R.D. (2003). *Motivating Students and Teachers in an Era of Standards*. Alexandria, VA: ASCD.

Schmoker, M., &Marzano, R.J. (1999). Realizing the Promise of Standards-Based Education. *Educational Leadership* 56(6), 17-21.

Shaywitz, S.E., Fletcher, J.M., Holahan, J.M., Schneider, A.E., Marchione, K.E., Stuebing, K.K., Francis, D.J., Pugh, K.R., & Shaywitz, B.A. (1999). Persistence of dyslexia: The Connecticut longitudinal study at adolescence. *Pediatrics*, 104(6), 1351-1359.

Shaywitz, S. (2003). *Overcoming Dyslexia*. New York, NY: Alfred A. Knopf.

Shanker, J.L. & Ekwall, E.E. (2008). *Locating and Correcting Reading Difficulties*, 8th edition. Upper Saddle River, NJ: Allyn and Bacon/Pearson.

Showers, J., & Joyce, B. (1996). The Evolution of Peer Coaching. *Educational Leadership*, 53(6), 12-16.

Simpson, M. (1995). Talk Throughs: A strategy for encouraging active learning across the content area. *Journal of Adolescent and Adult Literacy*, 38(4), 296-304.

Snow, C.E., Burns, S.M. & Griffin, P. (Eds.) (1998). *Preventing Reading Difficulties in Young Children*. Washington, D.C.: National Academy of Education.

Stiggins, R. J., Arter, J.A., Chappuis, J. & Chappuis, S. (2004*). Classroom Assessment for Student Learning: Doing it Right-Using It Well.* Columbus, OH: Assessment Training Institute, Inc.

Sousa, D.A. (2005). *How the Brain Learns to Read.* Thousand Oaks, CA: Corwin Press.

Tankersley, K. (2003). *The Threads of Reading: Strategies for Literacy Development.* Alexandria, VA: ASCD.

Tankersley, K. (2005*). Literacy Strategies for Grades 4-12: Reinforcing the Threads of Reading.* Alexandria, VA: ASCD.

Tankersley, K. (2007). *Tests that Teach: Using Standardized Tests to Improve Instruction.* Alexandria, VA: ASCD.

Toll, C.A. (2005). *The Literacy Coach's Survival Guide: Essential Questions and Practical Answers.* Newark, DE: International Reading Association, Inc.

Topping, D.H. & McManus, R.A. (2002). *Real Reading, Real Writing.* Portsmouth, NH: Heinemann.

Torgesen, J. K. (2009). *Preventing early reading failure and its devastating downward spiral.* March 3, Retrieved from https://www.ncld.org/at-school/general-topics/early-learning-aamp-literacy/preventing-early-reading-failure-and-its-devastating-downward-spiral.

Torgensen, J.K. (2004). Preventing Early Reading Failure. *American Educator*, Fall.

U.S. Department of Labor (2010). *Occupational Outlook Handbook,* 2010-11 Edition. Retrieved December 30, 2010, from https://www.bls.gov/oco/oco2003.htm.

Torgesen, J.K. & Burgess, S.R. (1998). Consistency of reading-related phonological processes throughout early childhood: Evidence from longitudinal, correlational, and instructional studies. In J. Metsala & L. Ehri (Eds.), *Word recognition in beginning reading* (pp. 161-188). Hillsdale, NJ: Erlbaum.

Torgesen, J.K., Rashotte, C.A., Alexander, A. (2001). Principles of fluency instruction in reading: Relationships with established empirical outcomes. In M. Wolf (Edward), *Dyslexia, Fluency, and the Brain*. pp. 333-355. Parkton, MD: York Press.

Vacca, R.T., & Vacca, J.L. (2008). *Content Area Reading: Literacy and Learning Across the Curriculum*. 9th Edition. Boston, MA: Pearson Education, Inc.

Vygotsky, L.S. (1978). *Mind in Society*. Cambridge, MA: Harvard University Press.

Wilde, S. (2000). *Miscue Analysis Made Easy: Building on Student Strengths*. Portsmouth, NH: Heinemann.

Willis, P., Bland, R., Manka, L. & Craft, C. (2012). The ABC of peer
mentoring – what secondary students have to say about cross-age peer mentoring in a regional Austrailian School, Educational Research and Evaluation, 18:2. Pgs. 173-185.

Wylie, R.E., & Durrell, D.D. (1970). Teaching Vowels through Phonograms. *Elementary English,* 47(6), 787-91.

Yoop, H. (1988). The validity and reliability of phonemic awareness tests. *Reading Research Quarterly*, 23, 159-177.

About the Author

Karen Tankersley is a long-time veteran of public-school service. Karen has served in many positions during her career, including teacher, coach, and K-8 principal. She has also served in various leadership positions at the district office level. She has consulted with school districts across the U.S. on school improvement and effective reading instruction.

Karen has an extensive language and language acquisition background, including a BA in French and a minor in German and English. She holds a Master of Arts in Reading and a Doctor of Philosophy degree in Educational Leadership.

In her early career, Karen spent 10 years as a classroom teacher, foreign language teacher, reading specialist, and teacher of the gifted and talented instructional coach. She is an expert on effective literacy.

After entering administration, Karen served for 13 years as a principal in schools recognized nationally for outstanding achievement and high academic performance. Karen was a curriculum director and senior leader in superintendent roles at the district level.

In addition to her public-school service, Karen has experience as a curriculum and professional development writer for national teacher preparation programs. For 2 years, she worked for a national publisher coordinating training services and professional development.

From 2007 to 2011, she served as a full-time faculty member in the Educational Leadership Department of Arizona State University, where she trained principals in effective school leadership.

Karen has published articles in several educational journals, including *Educational Leadership*. She is the author of *Threads of Reading: Strategies for Literacy Development* (ASCD, 2003) and *Literacy Strategies for Grades 4-12: Reinforcing the Threads of Reading* (ASCD, 2005) on effective strategies for reading instruction and *Tests that Teach: Using Standardized Tests to Improve Instruction* (ASCD, 2007).

More recently, she has been the author of Childhood Obesity: Helping Children Lead Fit and Healthy Lives (Little John, 2011); and 7 books for students in grades 4-8 called the Exploring Nature Series. Karen can be reached on her website: https://www.threadsofreading.com

Thank you for reading this book on coaching teachers in literacy instruction.

Before you go…

If you enjoyed this book, please go to *Amazon.com* and support this author's work by leaving a review of this book.

Helpful reviews of this book allow this author to keep writing and helps others benefit from learning more about how to support teachers as literacy coaches.

Thank you in advance for reviewing this book and sharing your thoughts and insights about literacy coaching.

Other Books by Karen Tankersley:

Threads of Reading: Strategies for Literacy Development

Literacy Strategies for Grades 4-12: Reinforcing the Threads of Reading

Tests That Teach: Using Standardized Tests to Improve Instruction

Childhood Obesity: Helping Children Lead Fit and Healthy Lives

The Exploring Nature Series (Grades 4-8)

Sea Turtles: Amazing Giants of the Sea (Book 1)

Discover the Koala (Book 2)

Amazingly Awesome Snails! (Book 3)

When Wood Turns to Stone: The Story of the Arizona National Petrified Forest (Book 4)

Kangaroos Down Under (Book 5)

The American Black Bear: Life in the Wild (Book 6)

www.ingramcontent.com/pod-product-compliance
Lightning Source LLC
Chambersburg PA
CBHW071415090426
42737CB00011B/1474